SCHOLASTIC
ART & WRITING AWARDS
PRESENTS

THE
BEST
TEEN
WRITING
OF
2016

Edited by
Madeleine LeCesne
2014 National Student Poet
2015 Silver Medal with
Distinction Portfolio Recipient

For information or permission, contact:
Alliance for Young Artists & Writers
557 Broadway
New York, NY 10012
artandwriting.org

Editor: Madeleine LeCesne
Director, Programs: Debra Samdperil
Managing Editor: Hannah Jones
Design Director: Meg Callery
Production Manager and Proofreader: Jean-Paul Bass
Copy Editor: Ingrid Accardi
Production Assistant: Tommy de Yampert

Front Cover: *Be Happy*, Drawing & Illustration by Ji Eun Yang, Grade 12, Age 17, University Laboratory School, Honolulu, HI

Back Cover: *Stand Strong*, Photography by Eli Dreyfuss, Grade 12, Age 18, G-Star School of the Arts, Palm Springs, FL

Inside Front and Back Covers: *Polarization*, Digital Art by Sophie Hullinger, Grade 12, Age 18, Alexander W. Dreyfoos School of the Arts, West Palm Beach, FL

DEDICATION

The Best Teen Writing of 2016 is dedicated to Ken Burns, who received a Scholastic Writing Award in 1971 for an essay titled "First Christmas in Ann Arbor" as a senior attending Pioneer High School in Ann Arbor, Michigan. He has since become an internationally renowned, award-winning filmmaker with an exceptional career spanning more than thirty-five years, having directed and produced some of the most acclaimed documentaries ever made, sparking important national conversations about race, health, morality, politics, and the heroes of our times.

The recognition Burns's work has received highlights his dedication and incomparable point of view. His films have collectively received thirteen Emmy Awards and two Academy Award nominations and, in 2008, Mr. Burns was honored at the News & Documentary Emmy Awards by the Academy of Television Arts & Sciences with a Lifetime Achievement Award. In 2016, he was appointed by the National Council on the Humanities as the Jefferson Lecturer, the highest honor the federal government confers for distinguished intellectual achievement in the humanities. Also in 2016, he accepted the Scholastic Art & Writing Awards' Alumni Achievement Award.

TABLE OF CONTENTS

ABOUT THE BEST TEEN WRITING OF 2016

The pieces featured in *The Best Teen Writing of 2016* were selected from works that earned National Medals in the 2016 Scholastic Art & Writing Awards. The Scholastic Awards, a national program presented by the Alliance for Young Artists & Writers, identifies and showcases teenagers with exceptional artistic and literary talent. Founded in 1923, the program celebrates the accomplishments of creative students and extends opportunities for recognition, exhibition, publication, and scholarships.

This year, 784 students earned National Medals in writing categories. The works selected for this publication represent the diversity of the National Medalists, including age and grade, gender, genre, geography, and subject matter. They also present a spectrum of the insight and creative intellect that inform many of the pieces.

A complete listing of National Medalists and online galleries of awarded works of art and writing can be found on our website at **artandwriting.org**. Visit our site to see how to enter the 2017 Scholastic Art & Writing Awards, as well as a list of our scholarship partners and ways you can partner with the Alliance to support young artists and writers in your community.

Some of the writing selections have been excerpted. Go to **artandwriting.org/galleries** to read all of the work as it was submitted.

ABOUT THE SCHOLASTIC ART & WRITING AWARDS

Since 1923, the Scholastic Art & Writing Awards have recognized the vision, ingenuity, and talent of our nation's youth, and provided opportunities for creative teens to be celebrated. Each year, increasing numbers of teens participate in the program and become a part of our community—young artists and writers, filmmakers and photographers, poets and sculptors, video game artists and science fiction writers—along with countless educators who support and encourage the creative process. Notable Scholastic Awards Alumni include Andy Warhol, Sylvia Plath, Cy Twombly, John Baldessari, Ken Burns, Kay WalkingStick, Richard Avedon, Stephen King, Luis Jiménez, Paul Chan, and Truman Capote—to name just a few.

Our Mission

The Scholastic Art & Writing Awards are presented by the Alliance for Young Artists & Writers. The Alliance is a 501(c)(3) nonprofit organization whose mission is to identify students with exceptional artistic and literary talent and present their remarkable work to the world through the Scholastic Art & Writing Awards. Through the Awards, students receive opportunities for recognition, exhibition, publication, and scholarships. Students across America submitted nearly 320,000 original works during our 2016 program year across 29 different categories of art and writing.

Our Programs

Through the Scholastic Awards, teens in grades 7–12 from public, private, or home schools can apply in 29 categories of art and writing for a chance to earn scholarships and have their works exhibited and published. Beyond the Awards, the Alliance for Young Artists & Writers produces a number of programs to support creative students and their educators, including the Art.Write.Now.Tour, the National Student Poets Program, the Scholastic Awards Summer Workshops and Scholastic Awards Summer Scholarships programs, the Golden Educators Residency, and much more. The Alliance publications feature works by National Medalists of both art and writing in our annual National Catalog. Additionally, we publish a collection of exemplary written works in this anthology, *The Best Teen Writing*, and a chapbook that features works from the National Student Poets. These publications are distributed free of charge to schools, students, educators, museums, libraries, and arts organizations across the country.

2016 SCHOLASTIC ART & WRITING AWARDS
NATIONAL WRITING JURORS

American Voices Award
Peter Blackstock
Breena Clarke
Marian Fontana
Alexandra Franklin
Liana Gamber-Thompson
Naomi Jackson
Mira Jacob
Catherine Lacey
Molly Parent
Ben Samuels
K-Fai Steele
Jordan Teicher

Best-in-Grade Award
Will Chancello
Anna DeVries
Bridget Read
Kerri Schlottmann
Leigh Stein
Kate Tuttle

Creativity & Citizenship Award
Michael Archer
Scott Saul
David Unger

Critical Essay
Rebecca Saletan
Leisel Schillinger
Kristin Strohmeier

Dramatic Script
Pat Fox
Josh Gondelman
Karolina Waclawiack

Flash Fiction
Cynthia D'Aprix Sweeney
Elissa Schappell
Justin Taylor

Gedenk Award for Tolerance
Antonio Aiello
Swati Khurana
Joel Whitney

Humor
Jazmine Hughes
Maris Kreizman
Eric Levai

Journalism
Michelle Dean
Lydia Denworth
Efrem Mindell Zelony

Personal Essay & Memoir

Rebecca Bondor
Caroline Casey
Tracy Cochran
Michelle Koufopoulos
Lisa Leshne
Rachel Reiderer

Poetry

Cheryl Clarke
Esther Cohen
Efrem Mindell Zelony
Jeff Shotts
Kristin Strohmeier
Michael Toujiline

The RBC "Flaunt It" Award

Abigail Donahue
Jason Reynolds
Andrea Worthington

Science Fiction & Fantasy

Shyla Bass
Amy Lawless
Daniel José Older

Short Story

Katharine Freeman
Lauren Holmes
Halimah Marcus
Lincoln Michel
Efrem Mindell Zelony
Stephen Sparks

Writing Portfolio

David Anderson
Faith Childs
Cordelia Jenson
Tracy O'Neill
Duvall Osteen
Lisa Shulman

EDITOR'S INTRODUCTION
Madeleine LeCesne
2014 National Student Poet
2015 Silver Medal with Distinction Portfolio Recipient

My least favorite piece of advice on writing: Write what you know. This adage feels as old as language itself, and anyone who has ever tried to write anything has heard it before. It's the first piece of advice most young people are given, the first voice that pulls us to the paper and asks that we take this seriously. Before we can even begin to write, we are asked to be brave, because writing what we know means being seen honestly and truly, even if we are the only ones who will ever read the words. This principle gives us permission, but not on our own terms. It tells young writers that their only authority lies in the life they've already lived, not the world they can create.

Many of the writers in this anthology seem equally as suspicious of "Write what you know" as I am. One poet's heart collects dead deer like lovers. Another takes on the voice of a wolf in a seedy Birmingham motel. A fiction writer juggles three different points of view: a seablue drag queen, his mother with hair like rope, and the lonely production guy who adores him. And although it seems as if these writers cannot possibly know what any of these situations is really like, we must trust them. Because there are others in this anthology who do write what they know, who write so bruisingly about being sexually assaulted that you cannot unfeel them; a critical essayist who tells you how she never knew the lives of Asian women, women like her, could be meaningful, because their stories rarely appear in the literature taught in American schools. A memoirist recalls flattening her breasts on the hardwood floor of her family home in the hopes of escaping her father's cancer diagnosis. And according to a poet, there is a classroom in New Hampshire where a girl sits with a Confederate flag hanging above her head during lessons every day. Each of these accounts marks a situation these young people shouldn't have to know. And yet they do.

The works in this anthology belong together not only because they were written by teenagers. They also commune here because they were written every day of these young writers' lives: in a house where daughters eat dinner in silence, the inside of a fish's stomach, the barrel of a shaking shotgun. Ava Goga puts it best in their poem "The Nosebleed Year": "We knew, somehow, every day of our lives / had led to this." Every day, somehow, led to these stories, essays, and poems. These writers wrote to find out what they knew. And now, their words are irrevocable.

NYANNA JOHNSON, *Mirrored Self*, Grade 12, Age 17, Stivers School for the Arts, Dayton, OH. Paula Kraus and Leah Stahl, *Educators*

GOLD MEDAL PORTFOLIO

Graduating high school seniors may submit a portfolio of four to eight works for review by authors, educators, and literary professionals. The eight recipients of the Gold Medal Writing Portfolio each receive a $10,000 scholarship.

Some of the writing selections have been excerpted.
Visit **artandwriting.org/galleries** to read all of the work as it was submitted.

peoplewatching

ALLISON JIANG, Grade 12, Age 17. Holmdel High School, Holmdel, NJ.
Steven Dante, *Educator*

There are times when I like,
when life is not too fast,
to sit on a bench in the corner of my mind and watch
the faces, like flags, like signposts
rush past like gods,
each as exciting as a new book to read.
And I wonder how we all fit
on this earth, so small
when there is so much big loving to be done.
I wonder these things and I cradle my heart in my hands;
The strangers roll around like marbles in a frying pan.
      There is a pretty green one. It looks like a cat's eye.
      Here's a big one. I wonder what his children are like.
I rub them into my skin for when life gets old.

What We Knew Then About Love (for her)

ALEX ZHANG, Grade 12, Age 17. Phillips Exeter Academy, Exeter, NH. Todd Hearon, *Educator*

I used to wonder if love worked like a shower. The usual day—I would walk into the bathroom, remove my clothing, feel the graze of the porcelain tub, hear the squeak of a knob. But this time, emotions would rain down upon me. I thought love was as sudden and overwhelming as the stream that sputtered out of the chrome head in my bathroom.

For a long time, I romanticized love and sex in that way. I fervently wrote desperate poems about desire, wondering when it would come to me. I read young romance novels detailing "fateful" gazes and unexpected roses. And sometimes in the quiet confines of my room, with a mixture of disgust and longing, I wondered about losing my virginity.

If only I had known then.

* * *

In fifth grade, there was porn. I still remember those boys huddled during recess, so close you'd think it was for warmth.

"Whoa, she's not even wearing a bra," Ryan said, adjusting his backwards hat to fix the loose blonde strands in front.

"Are boobs supposed to look that . . . saggy?" asked another boy, Matthew. "This feels wrong. I'm out of here." He shook his head as he walked off, kicking up woodchips.

"All I know is that I can't wait to do that," James proclaimed, putting his phone away. He looked over to the girls at the swing set with an unsettling enthusiasm.

"I mean, she looked sort of in pain," I mumbled, hiding half my face behind the boy in front of me. Even with my eyes closed, the woman's straining expression remained imprinted in my mind.

"What are you talking about? She loved it." James held the "o" slightly longer. He plucked a dandelion from the early spring grass, fiddled with it, and threw it back to the decayed yellow ground.

* * *

By my second year of high school, I'm still a virgin. Most of my peers are not. You are not. You're a pretty girl—soft brown hair, lips that look like they have gloss even when they don't, and big opal eyes. The other boys talk only about your body—thin legs with a "nice" gap, an hourglass waist, and large "perky" breasts. You've already had several boyfriends and a surplus of options. In most people's eyes, you're doing "well."

But we both wanted more; our childhood fantasies never died. I remember that day we talked about love and how we both needed it. We were in the park. On a splintered bench, we watched couples stroll past, their fingers interlaced. In my mind, the spaces between their clenched hands disappeared. They were meshing into one.

You turned to me. "I'm just so ready for something new," you sighed, half-smiling in that pathetic sort of way.

"Yeah, same," I laughed. But I lied—I didn't know what "new" meant.

* * *

I have always struggled with the word "sorry." Not now. I'm sorry I was not there for you the day after the park. Three floors up, I am talking about television over the phone; three floors down, you are being raped.

It's all a blur when I try to remember. You knock on my door and cry as you grasp me. Through your intoxication I try to piece together a story—you met him at a party, he seemed nice, you didn't want to go that far, you tried to text me, I didn't respond, you cried, he didn't use a condom—I almost throw up.

Even now, I need no reminder of the words he said—I am trying my best to forget. I am trying my best to forget how he took you with force; that there were bruises that stained for days. I am trying to forget all the things he made you say; words still caught like staples in your lips.

"I feel so dirty," you sobbed to me. You were crying so hard I could only hear wheezing. "So dirty." A hoarse whisper.

* * *

I cannot compare the pain. Days, weeks after, I pondered what I could relate it to. It was different than the time I fell and broke my ankle in the fourth grade. It was different than getting stitches in my forehead when I was eight. I couldn't fathom a pain that remained.

* * *

Even now, I sometimes imagine you back at home and wonder if you are showering. I wonder if you are still cleaning off the dirt from that night. You called me crying the day after and told me his face was imprinted in your mind. I cannot imagine how it feels to see him each time you close your eyes—you are falling again and again. You are hurting again.

* * *

I know better now. Each morning brings another trip to the porcelain tile of the bathroom. The showerhead is now broken, the water forcing down in a heavy, pelting gush. A jagged stream—I imagine the shots against my back are him. I know now it isn't love.

I am terrified you will never trust again. A bed in twenty years—I see you distant from your lover, gone to the bathroom to scrub off the grime. The bruises disappeared, but the memory did not.

* * *

Today I am eighteen and I am still a virgin. One sleepless night, I walk to my bookshelf and pull a book. It's a collection of fairy tales my mother used to read to me. I flip to a random page.

"In love and finally together, they lived happily ever after." I slam the blue plastic cover and hurl it onto my couch. I chuck pillows at it until it's buried in a pile of rumpled white. It was easier when I was younger. Often now, I try to draw the line between love and sex, but my thoughts are lost under soap bubbles and shower waters.

As I fall asleep, I hold my pillow between my arms and murmur comforts to myself. Do not worry, you will find love. Something good, something new will come. I rinse and repeat until my eyes shut. Do not worry, you will find love. Something good, something new will come.

But I lie.

Cats

RACHEL PAGE, Grade 12, Age 17. Woodrow Wilson Senior High School, Washington, D.C. Kathy Crutcher, *Educator*

My dog, who has no name, has begun to kill stray cats. He leaves them on our doorstep, bodies stiff like stuffed dolls, fur matted in the crescent moon of his teeth. The hairs his mouth have touched dry hard. Some have their eyes still open. The fringe of their eyelashes around the glassy surface makes them appear almost wild.

I am not sure how to explain this phenomenon. The first cat appeared without warning the day after my twenty-fifth birthday. I found it when I opened the door to grab the newspaper, its body curved around the doormat in a parenthesis. My dog poked his head through my legs to look through the doorway, as if he, too, were curious. Since my mother gave him to me as a puppy, he has developed a way of staring up at me with eggshell eyes in a way that makes it impossible to blame him. He once knocked over a glass of water I had placed on the arm of my sofa and produced such a sad, strange whining noise that I ended up apologizing to him instead of the other way around.

I admit it: I did not find anything concerning about the occurrence, the first time it happened. It is odd, yes, to have a dead cat show up on your doorstep. But I had noticed many strange things since moving into the house. There is a bird that lives next to my bedroom window and whistles the same two notes over and over, a sound eerily like a screaming child. The gate sometimes clangs open and shut, mostly on breezy days, but nevertheless, the noise is alarming. A dead cat was just one more addition to the list of the property's disconcerting features. I buried it in my yard under the forsythia bush, and when I woke up the next morning, yellow flowers had scattered themselves over the raw earth like apologies. I found this poetic.

The second dead cat was one that I knew, an orange tabby I often saw on my trips to and from the local municipal library. His face had always made me shiver, one eye brown and the other a too-light blue. I will not say that I was glad that he was dead; of course not. But it did bring me a certain relief, yes, to not feel his ghost eyes on me while walking to the library, to not have to turn around and look back over my shoulder to make sure he was not following me. I buried him in the yard next to the first one, twin hills that poked out of the earth like sores.

After the third cat, a steely blue-gray tom with a scar on his right shoulder, I began to question my dog's intentions. He had never behaved so strangely before; ever since my mother gave him to me, he had appeared to be the epitome of a normal dog, content with dozing in sunny corners and the occasional long walk. Yes, I admit, my first thoughts were immediately of my mother. It had to be she who had raised him wrong, in the seven months he spent at her house suckling from the old family dog. It was she, I was sure, who had awakened this carnal instinct inside of him, this lust for warm bodies and brittle bones. When she dropped off the dog at my apartment six years ago, she told me: "I want you to learn something from this, Andrew. A life is not the seven blocks between your apartment and the library, and to be honest I am concerned about you." It was after she died that I moved to my current house, twelve blocks from the library instead of seven, but I don't mind. In fact, I enjoy the walk.

In total my dog has brought twenty-three cat bodies to my doorstep. He leaves them in piles, one on top of the other, their bodies curled around each other as if in sleep. I dig circles of holes to bury them in until the grass is a graveyard piled with dirt and my hands are callused from shoveling. During my daily trips to the library, I check out books on cats and learn that their hearts beat almost twice as fast as those of humans. The first cat in space was French and had electrodes implanted in her brain. I imagine these once-living cats in space, the moon reflecting off of the orbs of their eyes, how their whiskers would float upwards like plants stretching toward the sun. Cats can survive falls of sixty-five feet, but not my dog's teeth on their neck, gentle like a surgeon. This won't hurt a bit.

It is after the twenty-third cat that I begin to lock the door. My dog, however, is impatient. He whines at me, scraping at the paint until there is nothing left but raw wood, scarred with the valleys of his nails. Surely he will be satisfied after the next cat, I tell myself, or the next. When I open the door, he is gone without looking back, flashing gray for a moment beside the wrought iron gate before disappearing into the street.

One night I stay awake in my living room, waiting for him to return. At 2:47 am his silhouette appears on the path outside my house. The cat is black with streaks of white, and he holds it by the neck like a mother carrying its kitten. He places it almost gingerly on the doormat before loping into the yard, where he will sleep under the forsythia bush as he often does, the branches curved around themselves in the shape of his body.

When I open the screen door, it creaks too loudly. The cat's left forepaw is curled as if batting at an invisible mouse. I reach down to touch it and am surprised by its warmth. My fingers move upwards to its throat and find a pulse. A pulse, yes, wavering but unmistakable—the cat is dying but not dead. The piles of cat books that crowd my bedside table have not prepared me for this situation. The pattern of blood against warm fur is like Morse code. I imagine that I see the cat's paw quiver, and I swear it is asking me to help it—this cat, whose salt-and-pepper fur reminds me of my mother, is asking me to finish the job that my dog started.

I take the flowerpot that sits beside the doorstep, and it is cold and almost moist in my hands. When I drop it, it is almost as though it has slipped through my fingers, just barely an accident. There is a crunch. A cat has two hundred and thirty bones in its body, twenty-four more than a human. I lean over the railing and throw up white and yellow among the purple of the flowers that have begun to wilt. The back of my throat burns. When I look up, my dog is staring at me from his place in the yard, his eyes glowing like twin stars.

I bury the cat the next day. There is no more space in my yard, so I dig into the flowerbed, leaving the asters naked and broken on the pathway. I cannot bring myself to clean the doorstep. I pat down the dirt around the grave and enter the house through the back door, which is rusted but does not smell of blood and musty fur and the sickly sweetness of crushed flowers.

At the library I go from the Zoology section to Social/Family Relationships. There are books on dealing with grief, on losing family members, on reconciling religion with the death of children who have never said their first words. They do not talk about what to do if your dog has become a murderer. *When*

Will I Stop Hurting? Dealing With the Loss of a Loved One, by an author whose name I can't pronounce, has a section on the death of a pet. You may blame yourself for the loss of your pet, it says. Remember: There is nothing you could have done. At the bottom of the page someone has scribbled: *Sometimes we never let go.* This feels somehow profound. I rip the page out and fold it into eighths so that it will fit in my pocket and leave the library without checking any books out.

The next night there are no cats. My dog returns to the yard empty-mouthed, snuffles around in the grass before settling underneath the forsythia. Yellow flowers catch in his fur like a garland. There are crickets chirping right outside my window, louder than I remember. I almost call out to my dog to come in but stop myself. When my mother came to my apartment to give him to me, I did not let her inside. She did not ask, and for some reason it never occurred to me to offer, and we stood like strangers in the doorway, relearning each other's faces. When I close my eyes, I can picture the way my dog stared at me from the garden as I lifted the flowerpot above the cat's head, as if telling me he knew I would. I do not want to forgive him. I close the curtains.

Cornflower Blue

RUOHAN MIAO, Grade 12, Age 17. Hamilton High School, Chandler, AZ.
Phyllis Carr, *Educator*

The summer the creek overflowed,
we watched as raw-skinned
boys shied
and shoved
each other with silt-blown hands into the
crack
of nature that had
beguiled the once unsullied earth.
We grappled with the
beer bottles, hushed cigarette stubs, the sun-swollen
days of greasing our palms in the dampened mud to create a
connoisseur's confection of sweat
and dirt, scuttling hands uncertain of the tangled
weeds beneath. Your father warns us
about the
journey through the stream, confirms his fears
with yellow gazette clippings of the last time
the river spilled over, its brim a
briny ten-gallon
hat pouring the excess into the fluted swell of
children's lungs.
I wonder if he knows about
the green boys, the fearless explorers,
the Columbuses and Vespuccis
whose scrappy legs sink ever
deeper
still.

Bad Ending

SHAYLA CABALAN, Grade 12, Age 18. Roncalli High School,
Aberdeen, SD. Cheri Anderson, *Educator*

My Uncle Jamie used to make me computer games in his free time.

Vividly I remember his musky scent, the sturdy way in which he balanced me between two hairy, tanned arms, the prickling sensation of his stubble rubbing against the top of my head, and how his fingers flitted effortlessly across the laptop keyboard despite being thick as sausages and callused from physical labor. These were the only memories of my childhood worth retaining, those long summer days when I would get to visit Uncle Jamie, who read computer codes the way most parents would read their children bedtime stories. For each of my rare visits to his little rundown apartment, he made a brand-new game for me to immerse myself in, and we would spend hours upon hours just sitting on his groaning striped sofa, me tapping away eagerly at his keyboard, him doing my hair and watching earnestly my adventures in whatever new, fantastic world he had created. Obviously, the games themselves were not exceptionally high quality and would glitch out nine times out of ten, but that was never what mattered, at least to me.

"Why do you make me games?" I had asked him one day after defeating a particularly difficult boss, and I felt his fingers still in my hair midbraid. Later on I would think about how Uncle Jamie's fat fingers belied his gentle nature, how he should have been out fighting crime like the heroes he created for me instead of sitting inside, dutifully making my games, meticulously braiding my hair, carrying me carefully to bed.

"To make you happy," he mumbled quietly after a long while, finishing the braid and tucking a flower behind my ear with a flourish. "The first time your mother dropped you off here, you wouldn't speak to me, no matter what I tried. You looked like you would cry every time I came close."

I nodded gravely. "You were big and scary."

I remember the way he chuckled at that, his barrel chest rumbling against my back. "Yes. And then I gave up, after countless attempts, and started working on a game, and all of a sudden, you were over my shoulder. Just like that. So I let you play through the trial, and you smiled for the first time ever. That's why I make you games."

"Teach me," I'd said, and his smile brought out his wrinkles and the crescents beneath his eyes.

"Okay."

Two years later, in the dead of night, a drunk driver folded Uncle Jamie in half, and he left me his laptop, his codebook, his hair ties, and nothing more. His last game he called Good Ending, and it went unfinished. I did not touch the laptop for months, and when I finally did, I gave the file a better, more appropriate name, but found that for all our lessons, I could never so much as open his final game—and even worse, could not delete it.

Words From Our Vegan Cave Tubing Guide

SOPHIA MAUTZ, Grade 12, Age 17. Lincoln High School, Portland, OR.
Lily Windle, *Educator*

The pink and purple morning glories you see
wrapped all along this barbed-wire fence
are like this morning—
dawn invading the dark
like a bursting star.

Farmers grow young cashew trees over there.
The fruit is actually very acidic; you have to boil it
to get that sweet taste of dried and salted wood.

I have a garden that I can only tend to
in April and May, when high season comes to a lull.
I grow cabbage. Sometimes I steam it,
other times I save it to make coleslaw.

See that sign that says "Tapir Crossing"?
You don't want to run into a tapir walking with its baby.
It will do anything to protect its child.

The central jail has a gift shop.
The inmates wear orange, just like in America.
They hang their dirty jumpsuits from the wires that crackle
up ahead.

A Taiwanese family bought this land
so they could farm dragon fruits.

I don't have any children.

When there are forest fires,
we don't get firefighters to put them out.
It is very common in Belize
to just let it burn.

You can eat the begonia leaves that grow from this trunk.
Rip the stem from its roots and suck—
they taste like sour apples.

Here, eat this too—
do you like the taste of the coquito nut?
It takes a lot of effort to break through its two layers
to get to the small milky egg in the center.

They say the water that drips down from these cave walls
is holy water—it is often collected in buckets
so that when babies are born, their umbilical cords
are washed in it.

The blackwood tree is poisonous. It has black sap.
The gumbo-limbo tree always grows right next to it.
Its white sap soothes whatever injury you can get from the
blackwood.
That's just how nature works.

Watch, watch how when you touch this cluster of plants
the spiral of leaves begin to close and play dead.
See how the green fan shuts in two sheer seconds.
See how afraid it is of your touch.

What Is a Feminist?

SYDNI WELLS, Grade 12, Age 17. Miami Country Day School, Miami, FL. Samuel Brown, *Educator*

Puberty was as confusing a time for me as anyone. When my body started developing, I was launched into a spotlight I had never asked to be put in to begin with. As a young black girl, I could look forward to broad, fleshed-out hips, thick thighs, and coarse hair. Growing up, I faulted none of them. The end of elementary school initiated battles of a body-image war I would struggle with for years to come. While my friends were able to project themselves into Hannah Montana, Lizzie McGuire, and every other teen girl on Disney Channel, I struggled to find a somewhat similar-looking role model who wasn't thin, with perfectly straightened hair, and big, round eyes. Once we hit our formative years, my best friend grew into a tall, slender silhouette that gave her long, wavy hair and fair skin, the rest of the perfect formula for boys' affection. I sat behind her and watched as countless admirers fawned over her perfectly flat stomach and delicate Anglo-American features. I grew to hate my body; my "chinky" eyes subjected me to relentless Asian jokes, jeans marketed to young girls from Hollister, American Eagle, and Gilly Hicks didn't even go past my knees, and my haunting stretch marks made sure I never, ever dared to change in front of any of my friends or family. I longed to be what every other girl around me seemed to be: skinny, confident, and white. Eventually I grew accustomed to my dad commenting on the size of my plates, reminding me habitually how much I was consuming and starting me on a precarious relationship with food. Lunch turned into an indulgence—food became a constant stressor every time friends asked me to come over, where I sat and prayed their parents wouldn't offer me anything to eat or ask me to have dinner with them. By the time I realized I wasn't going to naturally shed my "baby fat," it had grown into a much larger problem than I ever anticipated.

When I was old enough to understand what sex was, suddenly it was everywhere. I was projected into a sex symbol for men all over—my curves subjected me to experiences I violently resented, and by the time I was privy to the world of adultery, I had grown yet another toxic relationship with that too. There was a continuous tug-of-war between me wanting to healthily embrace my budding sexuality, and loathing the sexual object I had become. From then on I was suspended in an agonizing purgatory where I longed to be able to wear fitted cocktail dresses that actually made me feel good about my body, but was absolutely terrified of being exposed in any way that could leave me vulnerable to male attention. I forbade myself from going out in shorts or tank tops, developed a fierce phobia of being in public alone, and grew extremely wary of strangers.

This didn't just affect my social life, but extended into every aspect of my freshly impressionable teenage mind. Not only did I have a tumultuous relationship with my body, but I began to be ashamed of its power—a power I wasn't sure how to take back or own myself. Sure, I called it my body, but it never really felt like it was, and for a very long time I felt as if it was my responsibility to bear the brunt of unwanted advances, slimy gropes, and every uncomfortable compliment I could be subjected to from the imaginations of countless men.

As I struggled to find a comfortable balance between who I was currently and who I wanted to be, I embarked on an adventure of suffocating double standards. My guy friends recounted to me details of their numerous sexual escapades, bragging about the girls they "got with" and who they weaseled into sending them inappropriate pictures. When I complained about unsolicited "dick pics," I couldn't be taken less seriously and was made to feel guilty that I still refused to give in to male peer pressure. When I explored my own desirability in environments I was comfortable in and consented to, I faced the wrath of personal attacks by not only boys, but even girls my own age. My peers had branded me both a slut and a prude before I had the choice to consider either, and guys couldn't decide if I disgusted them or attracted them faster. When I had my first encounter with homosexuality, I was subjected to a different kind of scorn, where I unknowingly became every straight friend's peephole into a world they didn't want to accept but were desperate to understand. Some of my girlfriends swore I had become a different person than the one they changed with every other week before, and my guy friends considered me a circus attraction, because if my sexuality wasn't for their consumption, it was immediately rendered illegitimate.

A feminist is someone who believes in the sociopolitical and economic equality of the sexes. I have probably relayed that definition dozens of times in my entire life, and yet when I say the word it evokes so much more than a textbook Webster's definition. Feminism is the yellow brick road that became my salvation from any internalized misogyny I struggled with growing up, and showed me a world where I not only chose who and what I wanted to be defined by, but found a sense of belonging I had never been able to find anywhere else.

My guy friends will never know the humiliation of crying on a shopping-mall floor because two grown men had followed them across the mall, barking at them like some kind of bitch. They will never burn with resentment at their fathers for splitting up with them for just long enough for other men to see they were alone. They will never be afraid of shopping malls. But I will.

Life of Pi II

ADAM GOWAN, Grade 12, Age 17. Etobicoke School of the Arts, Toronto, Canada. Nicholas Morgan, *Educator*

I had always been an atheist. In all my life, I never questioned my religious beliefs. I saw religion as a way people justified their intolerance with primitive theories, which undermined the advances of modern science. I thought everything we needed to know could be understood through the scientific analysis of our sensory observations. There was no God.

I met Yann Martel in the summer of 2013. His wife worked with my dad, and I was pleased to have the opportunity to meet him, and tell him how much I had enjoyed the film adaptation of his novel, *Life of Pi*. In response, he told me to read the novel, half joking that it was better than the film.

In the beginning of the novel, Pi's uncle, who he calls Mamaji, says, "I have a story that will make you believe in god." In my reading, the story lived up to this claim. *Life of Pi* made me believe in god.

Since I was a child, I have been fascinated by mythology, and I loved stories with all my heart. However, it was only through my reading of *Life of Pi*, *The Golden Bough*, and Joseph Campbell's works of comparative mythology that I understood the value of these stories. I realized that if I viewed religious dei-ties as metaphors about life and existence, I could understand their purpose. It made sense to me, then, that religion was man's reaction to his instinctual fear of the unknown. This was the rich and beautiful origin of storytelling. I found God in my love of stories.

I wrote an essay about the transformation I had gone through and sent it to Yann Martel.

He wrote back, saying: "We are told two stories and we are invited to choose one to believe. That's it. Once you believe one story, the other falls to the side and doesn't play a role anymore."

This response puzzled me for a long time, and it was through the reading of various texts, including Nietzsche's *The Birth of Tragedy* and excerpts from the Upanishads, that I came to understand what he meant.

I realized, first, that all of creation could be reduced to the contrast of opposites: yin and yang, Apollonian and Dionysian, Brahman and Atman. I could see this in the biological process of sexual reproduction, and through artificial intelligence, in which every image, sequence of motion, or even mind can be reproduced in binary, as dots and dashes.

Second, I realized that these opposites are in fact in uni-ty. Man exists only in contrast to woman. Our eyes could not perceive the bright and colorful motions in film without black frames in between. Light is nothing without darkness, just as darkness is nothing without light.

Therefore, light and darkness are one, and darkness relies on both the absence and presence of light for its existence.

There is one Hindu concept, which illustrated for me, in a particularly poignant way, the truth of religion. This is the be-lief that the world we know, the physical world we observe through our senses, is Maya, illusion. This is revealed through the relativity of existence, which we see in its duality, and through impermanence. How can a world in which things exist only in contrast to other things, in which everything came from nothing and will inevitably return to nothing—be seen as anything but illusion?

Between the opposites, and in their unity, we find Brahman—the absolute, underlying unity of existence. Brahman is truth, and cannot be discovered through science, which only looks to the realm of illusion. Brahman can be found only by looking inward, as Atman, the individual soul, holds Brahman within. Existence is a game, in which Brahman hides within each of us, in you and me, and it is our job to turn inwards, and find that we are one with God.

NICHOLAS KILNER-PONTONE, *The Last Word*,
Grade 12, Age 17. George Washington Carver Center for Arts
and Technology, Towson, MD. Omead Afshari, *Educator*

GOLD, SILVER, AMERICAN VOICES, AND SPONSORED AWARDS

Students in grades 7–12 may submit works in 11 writing categories. This year more than 4,500 writing submissions that were awarded Gold Keys at the regional level were then adjudicated at the national level by authors, educators, and literary professionals. Gold, Silver, and American Voices Medals were awarded to works of writing that demonstrated originality, technical skill, and emergence of a personal voice.

Dedicated and generous sponsors of the Scholastic Awards make it possible for us to provide additional recognition and scholarships for select students who receive Silver and Gold Medals. We were pleased to add four brand-new sponsored award opportunities for students in 2016—The Herblock Award for Editorial Cartoon, The RBC "Flaunt It" Award, the Neiman Marcus Award for Fashion, and the Neiman Marcus Award for Jewelry—and to continue our ongoing partnerships with Bloomberg Philanthropies, and the Gedenk Movement.

Some of the writing selections have been excerpted. Visit **artandwriting.org/galleries** to read all of the work as it was submitted.

Hoping for Disaster

AMY DONG, Grade 12, Age 17. St. John's School, Houston, TX.
Linda Carswell, *Educator*

Our pop culture professor proposes the following scenario: A television ad shows a young family driving up a mountain to their winter vacation home. The father sits comfortably at the wheel, and the mother is turned around in her seat, talking with the two children. The rocky road winds and bends. Music from their stereo begins to escalate in intensity. What happens at the end of the commercial?

If you predicted something "bad" would happen—a car crash, ambulance noises, a warning to drive responsibly, death—you would be speaking for the vast majority of people who responded to this same question as part of a scientific study. And, along with the vast majority of people, you would be wrong.

Our professor goes on to tell us that the ad ends in a family reunion at their vacation home, with Christmas lights glowing on the rooftop, their car parked in the snow, and a warm holiday message paid for by an insurance company. But why do we expect the worst in the first place? According to our teacher, it is because we are "programmed in our narratives to expect disasters."

To test his theory, I skimmed the news for various headlines on November 11. These were the trending stories:

"Plane Hits Apartment Building in Ohio, Killing All on Board," "Band Breaks Up After 10 Years and 4 Albums Together-er," "Musician's Son Dies in Fall From Cliff After Taking LSD"

The next day, I repeated the experiment:

"Bodies of 7 Babies Found in German Apartment," "2 People 'Incinerated' in U.S. Airstrike Targeting 'Jihadi John,'" "Twin Suicide Bombing in Beirut Kills at Least 43 People."

After nine articles on death and destruction, I found one on the falling price of oil. After another seven, one on the benefits of coffee. Interesting, because the two articles that dotted an otherwise marred landscape of digital horrors were the only ones that I—or any average American—could actually relate to. Why was that? Perhaps because news that pertains to us is, more often than not, buried under a mountain of sensationalism. Perhaps because news outlets would rather drown us with disaster stories than let us swim through a sea of mundane events.

The pervasiveness of television has certainly contributed to our fascination with disasters. For decades, television has served as one of our main sources for "breaking news." It provides us with warnings about impending disasters and relays safety and recovery information. What makes this form of media so appealing, however, is not its objective presentation of facts but rather its sensationalized projection of reality. With its dramatic images and emotionally charged stories to capture our attention, television news has the power to convey—and sometimes even create—a sense of national significance. Large events such as September 11, Hurricane Katrina, and the Boston Marathon bombings always receive around-the-clock television coverage from cable news networks such as CNN, MSNBC, and Fox News. These broadcast outlets entice us to participate in the chaos without forcing us to face the repercussions, essentially distorting disaster into a paradox of terror and entertainment. We cling to catastrophe from the safety of our own homes, forgetting about the intricate realities of our own lives as we become transfixed by more extraordinary events.

The recent rise of social media only reinforces our culture of sensationalism. Today, 90% of young adults use social media, compared with 12% in 2005. At the same time, there has been a 69-point bump among those ages 30-49, from 8% in 2005 to 77% today. With the ability to present an unlimited amount of unfiltered information to such a large audience, social media now has the "power to define disaster." In this context, then, media sites such as blogs, photo- and video-sharing platforms, and social networks do not merely convey information about disasters. Instead, to compete for our attention, they blow disasters into hyperbolic proportions, hoping that their exaggerated coverage of any isolated event will shock us into sharing their photos, Tweeting their messages, and commenting on and liking their posts.

But with so many digital outlets constantly bombarding us with information, we can't help but feel drawn to sensationalized media. It is incendiary, offensive, stupefying, and enchanting. We know we don't need it, but we want it anyway to break up the incessant stream of white noise. Indeed, what we replay and share over and over again are not the stories related to our daily lives; they are the Vine videos that captured 6 seconds of the Boston Marathon bombings, the Facebook pictures that showed New Orleans in ruins after Hurricane Katrina, the dozens of news articles that detailed the graphic Ferguson shootings. By pointing out our obsession with disasters, I am not arguing that social awareness of disasters is intrinsically bad. I am, however, concerned with the disproportionate number of disaster stories we consume. By capturing our attention with exaggeration—startling headlines, shocking graphics, Twitter Moments, and Facebook's "trending" bar—sensationalized news essentially renders objective journalism obsolete. A simple presentation of facts may still be informative, but it will no longer interest us as we increasingly turn toward news presented in an emotionally charged, overembellished way. Following this logic, Haddow's ominous statement that the media now "defines disaster" seems all too justified. And that may be a disaster in itself.

Dearest Dining Room Chair: An Unapologetic Letter

NIA LARTEY, Grade 10, Age 15. Penn Wood High School, Lansdowne, PA. Joe Forsyth, *Educator*

First off, You should know this letter is not being written in Your presence. It was decided that would seem rather harsh, rather uncaring to do such a thing. Plus, it was much less awkward this way. Writing this letter with You in the room would just make the whole place stuffy and tension-filled and that would indubitably lead to small talk (also known as "off-topic" talk).

Ah, small talk. It always seems to distract a person, no? Always seems to slowly kill off confidence with the ever-rising volume of its song. One minute the immense amount of wasted pounds of food could be the impending problem at hand and the next the lost coupon for Kohl's half-off sale. And then before long I'd be like Sam Smith, talking to You maybe twenty times a day and still never getting a chance to say what I wanted to say. Speaking of dahling Sam, have You seen his new tats lately?

It would probably be in one's best interest to write this as a friendly letter—we're not strangers after all. Perhaps You should be asked how You are, what You're up to and all that.

Perhaps home-baked chocolate chip cookies should be attached with this letter. Perhaps I should throw in a "Just Thinking About You" card hinting of gingerbread and spice along with everything else. If it fits, it ships, right?

Ooooh! Better yet, instead of a letter—I'll just a give a speech! That way, I can say You "misheard Me" the whole time. That way I can apologize for all—if any—misunderstandings, and be on My merry way, acting as if nothing has happened. I can't do that when I send a letter. Sending a letter engraves all My words in stone. Sending a letter has Me swearing to God on top of Lincoln and Martin Luther King Jr.'s bibles. Sending a letter takes away My right to proclaim, "Oh, sorry! You must've misheard Me—apologies are mine!"

But I am not giving a speech. I am writing a letter.

Look, I know You all come in different shapes and sizes. You are the short, white plastic clearance-selling Home Depot chair and the sleek, blushing pink office one. You're a tall, smooth brown, a round, dirty, secondhand, and splintered orange stool, and a beat-up, bean-bag red.

And I'm—We're—speaking to all of You. Because You all need to hear Us.

The last time I talked to You was probably a couple of hours ago, maybe even just a few minutes. The details aren't all that clear—already running in with other encounters—but I still remember somewhat. She'd rush into the house, overwhelmed with the crushing groceries straining Her back and breaking Her shoulders, a three-foot human snake death gripped around her right ankle, or I'd set an Olympic record to get the phone for someone that asked Me to "fetch" it for them, or She'll mentally construct her to-do-list for the next week, or She'd trip over her feet to escape the violent hands of Her Dr. Jekyll—Mr. Hyde.

And then You happened.

We'd be on Our way, Our own problems at hand, and then Jericho would come tumbling down.

Sometimes We don't always fall flat out, face first, ankles twisted and veins rattled—and sometimes We do. Sometimes We replay the epic, off-the-Richter-scale earthquake in Our head slow-motion style and trip and fall again—and sometimes We don't.

We get hot, embarrassed even if we are Our only company. We instinctively say, "Sugar!" or "Shit!" or "Oww, damn it!" even if it didn't hurt all that much. We say, "Sorry" or "My fault" or "Oh, honey, are You okay?!" Then We'll tuck You back, straighten You up—perhaps Ourselves as well—and be on Our way, not even realizing We were talking. To. A. Chair. An inanimate object. A lifeless article. A clear sign of insanity. No, this does not mean You aren't living—You clearly are. But often whenever We talk to You—specifically during Our vigorously said apologies—You become lifeless and inanimate; You don't even bother to listen.

See, rarely do We not apologize. Rarely do You not take up so much of Our mind, so much of the apologies We give in Our whole lifetime.

Before it wasn't as prominent. If We were with someone they wouldn't question Our absentminded choice of talking to a chair, probably regarding it as stress or kids or "that" boss or colleague at work. Now, though, now it's a daily thing. Now it's natural. Sentences that could've been mixed and baked without the word now cool with "sorry" iced and sprinkled all over. We see You and think about the inevitable physical confrontation and proclaim "sorry" before Our big toe begins to even throb. We utter "sorry" to the pencil we drop, to the person who runs into a door and laughs at themselves, to the one who forgot their homework at home. We even voice Our utmost and deepest apologies to the person who pushes Us, or shoves Our arm off of the armrest. "Sorry" is Our everything. It's Our comforting word, Our gasp, Our question, Our remark, Our comment, Our sigh, Our amazement, Our surprise, Our conversation starter, Our I-Just-Wanted-to-Speak-Half-of-My-Mind-and-Give-Half-of-My-Opinion-But-Don't-Want-to-Come-Off-as-a-Bossy-Rude-Bitch safe word.

With "sorry" being all of these things, what does it mean, anyways? Well, Merriam-Webster's defines "sorry" as "feeling sorrow, regret, or penitence." To go by this definition would mean that I—and many others—are sorrowful or penitent toward thousands of things a day. Key word: things. (Don't believe me? Ask the Rug underneath You when the last time they apologized to a chair was and You'll see). University of California, Berkeley, linguist and best-selling author Robin Lakoff perfectly defined "sorry" when saying: "Sorry is a ritualized form meaning something like, 'I hope this is OK with you.'" If you were to ask Us, We'd define "sorry" as a jack-of-all-trades, the new Dumbing-Herself-Down-for-That-Guy word.

Now there are different theories as to why We're more prone to do this than You are. According to a June 23, 2015, *New York Times* article, there are reasons why I'm constantly apologizing to You. See, I tend to have a "lower threshold for what constitutes offensive behavior." In layman's terms, You're just as willing to apologize as I am: You just have a higher threshold (starting point) for as to what You think You need to apologize for. Things that I feel I have to apologize for— such as seeing someone else crack the screen of their phone with their butt—You don't feel like You have to apologize for. When someone says "Excuse Me" to Me, when I can't get a colicky baby to stop crying, when someone asks Me to please put in My earphones—all things I feel obligated to apologize for—and all things You probably wouldn't even associate the word "sorry" with.

Then there's gender linguist Deborah Tannen, who argues Your lack of use of the word is the result of You just not wanting to admit You're wrong. "Like a wolf baring its neck or a dog rolling over on its back," she writes, "an apologizer is taking a one-down position." And she's right. It's no secret the apologizer in any situation (usually) takes the role as the loser, the resigner. I absolutely hate losing, and apologizing is one of the most ultimate ways to say "I lost" without saying "I lost." Yet for as much as I hate losing, You'd never know I love winning by the way I always find Myself apologizing for My win—especially if it's over You. I feel as if I must not injure your self-esteem, that I must instead nurture it and protect it and never let its iron neck out of the crook of my arm. Yet, in order to do so, I must lower the magnitude of My win to a point where You can barely hear the Earth tremor, to a point where You claim My fame and glory.

Now, it's not necessarily Your fault We do this—it's all of Ours. The women in My life have apologized repeatedly for things they didn't need to, let alone should have. If I fell, for example, and scraped My knee after frequently being told to run in My little girl "high"-heels, it was always, "Oh, I'm so sorry, baby! Are you okay? Oh, I'm so sorry, you poor thannggg! Done gone and tore your stocking and scraped up God's knee, I'm sorry, child. C'mere and have a sip of my here soda, I'm sorry. I'm sorry, mmhmm, it's OK, baby." They didn't fall and scrape their knee—I did (and if I had listened, maybe I wouldn't have gotten hurt). Yet here they were breaking their backs to apologize to a five-year-old—let alone friends, guests, spouses, or bosses! And at the time, I didn't think much of their apologies because, hey, special treatment.

But you don't get special treatment when you're fourteen, fifteen, sixteen. It's rules from here on out at seventeen, eighteen, nineteen. In fact, a lot of You believe that it's "My place" to be the one apologizing, to be the one who's sorry even when I'm not the one at fault. I apologize to You at least fifty times a day, and I've yet to come across two of You that question my needless apologies in a single day. True, it is my fault, also—I shouldn't be apologizing in the first place. I should have confidence in Myself and not have a need to apologize for others and their actions—specifically when no apologies are needed.

It's hard, though, to break habits—especially those which deal with your vocabulary. I'm trying, though. After all, I did learn this habit. I wasn't born apologizing to the doctor when I didn't come out crying. I'm even learning to catch myself . . . just after "SORRY!" has already burst from My lips.

It's been very hard, You should know, to not apologize repeatedly this whole time. To not say, "Dearest Dining Room Chair, I'm sorry for declaring to not say sorry" even though I am exactly the opposite. The fact that You get mad at the one who bears children, at the one who has been oppressed generation after generation, while You say nothing to he who is "the breadwinner"—has kept Me to hold My tongue with a fist-like grip to forbid it from voicing any apologies. To he who is the math whiz, the soccer star, the mastermind of video-game consoles—it's fine that they don't apologize. They, they kick You and throw You to the side of the room. They dirty You up and they step on You and forget they've done it all in less than three seconds. Yet You say nothing, maybe You even smile. Maybe You whisper, "Boys are boys" while pushing aside painful, newborn splinters, forever trying to ignore the fact that You can't take the blows like You used to.

Back in 2014, Pantene asked a very important question: Why Are Women Always Apologizing? And though there are many answers to this question—We don't want to be labeled bitchy, We don't want to seem too smart, We don't want to be too mean—at the end of the day the same conclusion amounts to all of them: the "Sorry" epidemic needs to be eradicated. I've—We've—had enough of it. We can't apologize our way to the top jobs, to president, or to CEO. We can't apologize our way to equal wages, to fairer opportunities. All the girls behind us, the girls in future generations, need to know you don't have to apologize for everything. That you don't have to say "Sorry I'm always late" when you mean "Thanks for waiting." That you don't have to say "Sorry I'm not making a lot of sense" when you mean "Thanks for getting me." That you don't have to say "Sorry I'm just rambling" when you mean "Thanks for listening to me." Sorry is not the new Thank You, and they need to know you don't have to apologize for existing. Yet how will they do that if We keep apologizing for asking questions or standing somewhere or even for being indecisive?

It's so hard to be something you can't see. In this case—an unapologetic female.

And so, Dearest Dining Room Chair, I say it. Because the cycle needs to be broken. Because I'm tired of trying to find security in a two-syllable word. Because I'm completely over wasting my precious breath on the word "sorry" a million times a day.

Dearest Dining Room Chair, You will be hearing "Sorry" from Us no longer.

Conversion Therapy: Legalized Torture

PETER WENGER, Grade 8, Age 13. Home School, New York, NY.
Erin Dolias, *Educator*

Leelah Alcorn was a 17-year-old transgender girl who committed suicide on December 28, 2014. In her suicide note she talks about the struggles of being a transgender girl and having unsupportive parents. A major part of her struggle was her parents' refusal to allow her to transition and insistence that she undergo conversion therapy. Conversion therapy is a range of treatments that some believe can successfully make homosexuals become heterosexual and transgender people become cisgender (someone who associates with the gender he or she was assigned at birth). In response to Alcorn's death, a petition was started urging legislation banning conversion therapy; this petition got so much attention that the Obama administration said it will support efforts to ban conversion therapy.

Conversion therapy, performed by for-profit businesses, uses physical and mental processes to try to change someone's sexual orientation and/or gender expression. They do this by having the man a) play sports and avoid activities considered homosexual, such as going to the opera and/or art exhibits, b) avoid women unless for romantic reasons and increase time with straight men, and c) engage in heterosexual sex, enter into a heterosexual marriage, and father children—all while going to church. A large part of any conversion is to let that person know that their "behavior" is unacceptable. Baptist pastor John MacArthur believes as a part of the treatment parents must reject their homosexual kids: "You have to alienate them. You have to separate them. You can't condone that. It's inconsistent with a profession of Christ. You isolate them. You don't have a meal with them. You separate yourself from them. You turn them over to Satan." In some extreme cases children are subjected to aversion treatment. Aversion treatment is a controversial method of creating negative associations with the "undesirable" behavior. This has been used for alcohol and cigarette addictions as well as being gay. Aversion treatment when used in homosexuality can include ice blocks being placed on your hands, hot coils that can be turned on and off being wrapped around your arms, nausea-inducing drugs being injected into your system, and even the month of hell, which consists of tiny needles being stuck into your fingertips and running an electric current through said needles. All while pictures of men hugging, holding hands, and/or engaging in explicit acts are shown to you. The goal is to make the "patient" associate contact with men in general with pain and vomit. Supporters of this treatment believe that this will subsequently make the "patient" become straight.

Supporters of conversion therapy rely on a 2003 article by Dr. Robert L. Spitzer called "Can Some Gay Men and Lesbians Change Their Sexual Orientation? 200 Participants Reporting a Change from Homosexual to Heterosexual Orientation." Dr. Spitzer, who for most of his career was a professor of psychology at Columbia University, explains that his results show that some homosexual adult volunteers reported a change on the Kinsey Scale, also called the heterosexual-homosexual rating scale. Conversion therapy activists have taken this study and have used it to justify forcing conversion therapy on unwilling teenagers, even though this study used volunteering adults. This study is also problematic because it relies on self-reported change, and as we know, self-reported narratives are not entirely reliable. Even Dr. Spitzer has said that in no way, shape, or form does his study justify forcing conversion therapy on unwilling teens.

Fortunately, eighteen states are trying to pass laws that make conversion therapy illegal. Last year, legislators in a number of states, including New York, Michigan, Minnesota, Maryland, Wisconsin, and Vermont to name a few, proposed but failed to pass laws banning conversion therapy. Not only that, but legislators in Oklahoma are "moving to make conversion therapy for children emphatically legal." Emphasis on legal. Now you may be asking yourself, "What can I do to make sure that conversion therapy becomes illegal in all fifty states?" Well you can't do much to make sure a ban passes in all 50 states, but the more we talk about it and spread the word, the more likely it is that our state will pass a ban. It's frustrating that we even have to do anything to make sure that our representatives ban conversion therapy. You'd think it would be a no-brainer, but apparently it's not. Talk about it. Tell your family, tell your friends, tell everyone. I think Laci Green summed it up best: "How many Leelah Alcorns will find themselves alone and broken on the side of the road unable to take it anymore? If we're serious about equality and treating each other with humanity, then conversion therapy, and especially conversion therapy forced on minors, needs to stop."

On Diversity in the English Curriculum

JENNIFER LEE, Grade 12, Age 17. Hunter College High School, New York, NY. Alex Berg, *Educator*

"You know that game? Chinese telephone?"

My ninth-grade English teacher stands before the chalkboard, awaiting a response. Nobody responds. Finally, a student speaks up: "I think it's just called telephone."

Our teacher tries to explain himself, saying, "Well it's telephone, but it's called Chinese telephone because Chinese is gibberish."

This time, nobody corrects him.

To this day, that moment haunts me. It had never before occurred to me that a teacher could stand in a classroom that is 50% Asian-American and yet still say something so obscenely self-centered and racist. It had also never occurred to me before how thoroughly those students whose stories do not fit the dominant culture's narrative of the heterosexual white boy have been shut out of English class. Every single book we were taught that year was written by a dead white man: *Romeo and Juliet*, *The Catcher in the Rye*, *1984*, *Great Expectations*, and *All Quiet on the Western Front*.

Kids learn fast. Students of color don't need to be sat down daily and told explicitly, "Your story is worthless. Your heritage is worthless. You are worthless," for them to internalize this message. We just need to go to class, where we are told that the only stories that matter are ones about straight white men. Because ultimately, that is what the English department is telling students who have been marginalized by the curriculum—that the stories of your people do not exist, and you do not exist either. By establishing the normative narrative as that of the heterosexual white male and the white body as pure and generic, unmarked by the weight of a racial identity, the English curriculum pathologizes the bodies, stories, and lives of students of color as Other.

Writers like Toni Morrison and Amy Tan have fought to be heard, and they hold an invaluable place in English curricula because they show students the potential for change. *The Joy Luck Club* was not my favorite eighth-grade English book, but it was by far the most important to me—not because I related to the narrative itself, or even because I enjoyed the story, but because my teacher described Tan's writing as "beautiful." I had never studied a book by an Asian-American writer before. It had never occurred to me that the lives of Asian-American women—that the life of someone like me—could be worth reading or writing about. And it had never before occurred to me that the writing of an Asian-American woman, of a daughter of two immigrants, could ever be considered "beautiful."

Chekhov's Assault Rifle

JACKSON EHRENWORTH, Grade 10, Age 15. Avenues: The World School, New York, NY. Daniel Mendel, *Educator*

In the gentle warmth of early spring, before anyone realized that what was happening here was the near end of something much bigger, a tall girl stumbled to a row of desks, trying to fit herself into the small space. She was gasping and crying. Blood flecked her face, flung from the bodies of her friends and classmates. A silver ring pierced her brow, and the metal glistened in the cool light of the library. It also called attention to her. Though she was no more than seventeen, she carried the knowledge of her dying friends in her heart, a terrible pain that stopped her breathing. Without speaking, for that would have called attention to herself, the girl tried to make herself smaller. Her brown, frantic eyes were desperate. Please, they seemed to beseech, don't. Please don't. In a shooting, the victims speak with silent pleas.

Beyond the girl, on the edge of her vision, was a warren of desks and computers. Behind them, a boy with a shotgun was removing his trench coat. Eric Harris, a co-author of this particular massacre, stalked toward the brown-eyed girl. He paused though, as if distracted, and gently called out, "Peeka-boo." A second was all he spared for the golden teen hiding under the desk. That was all it took to pull her out and shoot her in the head, killing her instantly. The shotgun kicked back, breaking his nose, spraying his blood to mix with that of the dying girl. Then he was at the brown-eyed girl, asking her, "Do you want to die?" How was a teen to answer that? What should she have said to the boy with the shotgun, who had killed seven of her classmates, four before her eyes? It was a scene that was, at that time, incomprehensible to the modern mind.

School shootings are death by violence, taking away the rights of the victims to live. These deaths are not the result of accidents or natural disasters. They occur because people live in the hollows of hate. They occur because people can, with ease, gather bullets, and shotgun shells, and assault pistols, and automatic weapons. In the modern world, the death of children is, by and large, preventable. When it occurs, it represents our society's collective malfunction.

It was thirteen years later that the young first-grade teacher heard shots in the hallway outside her classroom. She was a substitute. She was just a child herself during Columbine, but the echoes of it knocked around in her memory. She did not hesitate, and she hovered behind her first-graders protectively as she tried to fit them all into the small classroom bathroom. She was not, not nearly, quick enough. He killed them all. The young substitute, and the fifteen first-graders. And then he gathered up his assault rifle and went to look for more.

Gun regulations have to change in this country, which means changing the discourse around gun control. That means taking on the gun lobbies, who wield enormous financial and political leverage and control the narrative around gun ownership. This year alone, the U.S. gun industry expects $11.7 billion in sales (Plumer, 2012). There is clear incentive within the industry to maintain the status quo of open access to any weapons, even if they are used for mass killing. To achieve any change, we have to change the discourse around gun control. It's hard to talk about guns without the argument being distorted into "people should be allowed to have guns," and "people should not." That is the narrative the gun lobbies promulgate—an imagined story of the government taking all privately owned guns away from citizens who want them for sport, to hunt, or to protect their homes.

The narrative that the government wants to confiscate guns is compelling, but it isn't one that advocates of gun regulations are making. Instead, this argument is a deliberate oversimplification on the part of vested interests (like the National Rifle Association) that is oddly seductive for those who should be more rational. The question that should be posed (that is rhetorical, as it's not a real question at all) is: Should any person be allowed open access to any and all assault weapons, or should some sensible regulations limit access to weapons of mass killing and institute background checks for all gun owners? I hesitate to use a president's name, because too many otherwise rational citizens flinch from bipartisan thinking, but let's name these regulations as what a president grieving for shot-to-death first-graders and college students called them: "sensible" gun laws and "responsible" gun ownership.

The first challenge with getting people to support sensible gun laws is getting people to care at all, and to do that we have to break through layers of lassitude, disinterest, and automatism. When you look at moments when support for responsible gun ownership has spiked, it has been after every mass shooting: Columbine, Virginia Tech, Fort Worth, Tucson, Aurora, Newtown. According to the Roper Center for Public Opinion Research, after each of these shootings, support for gun control gained traction—for a limited time. These mass shootings capture the public's attention. It might be because so many die all at once. It might be because the shootings happen in ordinary places. It might be because it is often a stranger who commits these acts, and so they feel threatening to all of us. At least for the few days after, these killings stay in the front of our minds. And we should feel threatened, for ourselves and our loved ones. Let's look at the sheer number of deaths in 2015. According to *The New York Times*, the U.S. is now averaging one mass shooting—which is a shooting in which at least four people are shot—per day. Malcolm Gladwell argues that the problem will become exponential. Shootings are becoming socialized; we have normalized a higher level of violence. That means the odds have never been stronger that someone you love will face a shooter, perhaps tomorrow, in your mall, or in your movie theater, at your kids' school, or in your classroom. Yet somehow, we spend little of our collective will to end this trouble.

U.S. lawmakers are capable of coming together in bipartisan ways. It just takes a tremendous event to make that happen. Congress responded to September 11th with a huge increase in funding and task forces. Most Americans fear terrorism, and most are willing to work together to fund anti-terrorism efforts, to pass laws aimed at protecting citizens, even to invade other nations. We take our shoes off in airports, we limit our possessions when we travel by air, and we acquiesce to expanded surveillance of U.S. citizens. We are willing to compromise our liberties, inconvenience ourselves, all to protect our loved ones and ourselves from potential violence at the hands of the fanatical and unstable. Somehow, though, domestic gun violence simply doesn't capture the collective will in the same way Al-Qaeda does. Yet the number of deaths from terrorism is in the low thousands, even including September 11th. Deaths from gun violence in this country are in the hundreds of thousands. Both CNN and Fox News (organizations which rarely report the same statistics), presented this comparison of deaths by terrorism vs. gun violence in the last decade: Since 2004, there have been 313 deaths by terrorism on U.S. soil. In the same period, there have been 316,545 deaths from gun violence. There are two things that should shock you in these statistics. The first is how many kids and adults have died from gun violence in the last five years alone. The second is how large that number is compared to how few deaths there are from terrorism. We spend billions on anti-terrorism, and we change what we can carry and how we can travel. Yet we can't agree to take even modest steps to control gun violence. It would be ridiculous if it weren't tragic.

Fear Itself

DANIEL WU, Grade 10, Age 15. Timber Creek High School, Orlando, FL. Catherine Melton, *Educator*

In the wake of a horrible attack on Paris, in an age where it seems new threats are called in daily, the political forum is understandably abuzz with discussion of how best to "win" the "War on Terror." It seems that every one of us exists in a cultural milieu of fear; our TVs are constantly calling out new horrors, every unknown face presents an unknown risk, and each tick of a clock reminds us of our mortality.

The fact of the matter is, the War on Terror started far before the events of 9/11. From the first of us to the last of us, we are each engaged in our own War on Terror. The emerging narrative of our byzantine machinations to defeat fear, a veritable spiderweb of justification, oppression, and voluntary blindness, has never made the call for change so fierce. From the first civilizations onward, fear, the emotional equivalent of our physical appendixes, has created and continues to create a sprawling butterfly effect of institutional quandaries: racism, sexism, heteronormativity, and elitism, just to name a few, and continues to perpetuate worldwide issues, such as global warming, world hunger, and indeed, the colloquial "War on

Terror." Surely some fears are helpful, but the ongoing, unending, in fact, accelerating, impacts of our progressive fear of the Other must be combated. It seems that a consilience of fields points to one conclusion: This fear is redundant and damaging.

What is fear? We cannot look to a simplistic, "common sense" definition. Fear is best comprehended as a subconscious avoidance of perceived threats, a state of being in which threats are dismissed in varying ways, positive and negative. At its root, fear is anchored in an ancient biological response. Johnson, a reporter with Discover, explains, "[Fear causes us] to display defensive behavior in response to threatening stimuli . . . fear turns out to be one of the most essential techniques that natural selection stumbled across to increase the survival odds of organisms in an unpredictable environment . . . For people who have undergone serious trauma . . . memories of fear can sometimes play a dominant role in shaping personality." The sum of our everyday interactions, our personalities, are constructed within an environment of our fears, and therefore our fears underlie each tenet of our modern societies. Fear is thus an antique of a hunter-gatherer existence—a nod to the primal past of our species, from times where every shadow hid wolves, where every unknown was a danger. However, humanity is no longer facing hungry wolves or angry bears; the world around us is safer relative to our hunter-gatherer past. Our greatest resource competitors? Ourselves. Food has transformed into jobs, wealth, and success, while bears and wolves have transformed into Others. The fear that once unified humanity against perilous nature has transformed into a wedge. As Lars Svendsen, professor of philosophy puts it: "A paradoxical trait of the culture of fear is that it emerges at a time when, by all accounts, we are living more securely than ever before in human history."

What of the Other? The Other is just that: the other. A wild card, an unknown, and thus, an implicitly perpetuated threat. Humans, listening to an age-old, species-ingrained mandate, fear what they do not know, what is unfamiliar, alien, different, and separate. Other. Hegel, in *The Philisophical Propaedeutic*, describes it as such: "I am a being for itself which is for-itself only through another. Therefore the Other penetrates me to the heart. I cannot doubt him without doubting myself, since self-consciousness is real only in so far as it recognizes its echo in another." The Other, in Hegel's view, is thus essential, and inherent in the Self—required to maintain its Selfness. Without it, self-consciousness cannot be achieved.

Applied culturally, this concept takes on a different spin. We, through the lens of the Other, analyze our own social identities and groups, and question our assumed superiority, our need to feel successful, accepted, and defined. To ensure superiority, we are urged, nay, required, to ensure that the Other, the metric and lens by which we measure ourselves, is inferior. A crusade must thusly be leveraged against the Other within civil society: a grand campaign to oppress, marginalize, and subjugate. Human schadenfreude in its everlasting glory.

In an effort to identify and secure Self, we look at the Other and fear it. We fear its inscrutability, its distinct nature, its "differentness." This response, encoded in our very substance, manifests in an ardent drive to assert dominance. In response to such a fear of the alien, of the unknown, or such a crisis of self-identity, we seek to gain security by ignoring, demonizing, and destroying the societal Other. In this way, we classify the other, we assume it is understandable, inferior, and thus, without threat. We cognitively negate fear of the Other by percolating it through a sieve of mediocrity and oppression. Fear has always pushed humanity to atrocity, in hopes of achieving "security."

Simone de Beauvoir puts it as such: "The category of the Other is as original as consciousness itself . . . Varuna-Mitra, Uranus-Zeus, Sun-Moon, and Day-Night . . . Good and Evil, lucky and unlucky auspices, right and left, God and Lucifer. Otherness is a fundamental category of human thought. Thus it is that no group ever sets itself up as the One without at once setting up the Other over against itself. If three travelers chance to occupy the same compartment, that is enough to make vaguely hostile 'others' out of all the rest of the passengers on the train. In small-town eyes all persons not belonging to the village are 'strangers' and suspect . . . Jews are 'different' for the anti-Semite, Negroes are 'inferior' for American racists, aborigines are 'natives' for colonists, proletarians are the 'lower class' for the privileged." Seen from this angle, it becomes readily apparent that racism, sexism, elitism, and other forms of oppression seem to form from a common spring: A jagged primal dread of the unknown, and a need for self-validation, accompanied by a base refusal to accept the humanity of others and to promulgate an ethic of care in our worldly affairs. In psychology, the analogous phenomenon is the In-group, Out-group effect. All summated, it is Fear of the Other.

And yet, this bleak picture is also shortsighted. With every social Self, of any size, there is its social Anti-Self, an Other. The West calls it the East, the North from the South, and Blue the Red. Sunnis and Shias, Whites and Blacks, We and They, I and You. Violent cycles within cycles, nesting dolls of hate and unity, spirals neverending. Even as We unite, We divide—Social Selves overlapping, contained in niches of an ever-sprawling complex of divisions and unions. With such an intricate complex of loyalties acting on each individual Self, oppression, discrimination, and persecution become expected on every scale. Global divisions retard global solutions, resulting in

American Exceptionalism, economic warfare, and the gradual rise of nationalism within the global arena. Yet humanity can abolish these crises and burn down the overhead burdens of our own creation. Reject the inherent fears humanity holds, and accept all as Selves, instead of Others.

Our society is afflicted with appendicitis. Humanity needs a mindframe shift, a determined rejection of the Otherizing fear apparatus within our societal consciousness, to move forward as a species. Only after society counters the root problem, only after we nullify the backdrop of fear in which we operate, do we have a chance of enforcing enduring solutions to societal oppression and global issues. I leave you with this: Do we really have to fear Fear itself?

Suckerpunch Sexism

BRITT ALPHSON, Grade 11, Age 17. Marymount High School
Los Angeles, Los Angeles, CA. Kate Hackett, *Educator*

EXT. ROOFTOP OF SCHOOL BUILDING—DUSK

PETER ABEL, 18, sits alone with only raggedy boxing shorts
on, looking triumphant.

PETER (V.O.): I won.

INT. KITCHEN—DAYTIME (3 MONTHS EARLIER)

PETER sits eating breakfast with PETER'S MOM, reading a
newspaper in disgust.

PETER: Jesus . . . did you hear about this, Mom? 120 boys in
Nigeria were taken captive by terrorist groups on their way to
school this morning.

PETER'S MOM flips through the newspaper, uninterested
and disengaged.

PETER'S MOM: Shame.

PETER: There are still people who actually believe boys shouldn't get an education. It's archaic.

PETER'S DAD sits down at the table.

PETER'S DAD: Hey, Peter.

PETER looks up and is instantly soothed by the sight of his father.

PETER: Hey, Dad.

PETER'S DAD: I can't believe it's your last year of high school. How did my little baby get so big?

PETER (V.O.): My father is a very emotional man.

PETER'S DAD starts to tear up.

PETER: Dad . . . stop.

PETER'S MOM: Let's get going, you're gonna be late for school. And I have to get to the office early.

PETER (V.O.): My mother is not.

PETER'S MOM gives PETER'S DAD a kiss on the cheek. PETER and PETER'S MOM exit.

EXT. SCHOOL PARKING LOT—DAYTIME

PETER walks up to his best friend MAX and they do a guy handshake/hug.

PETER (V.O.): This is Max, my best friend. I'm hesitant to call him that. I've known him since we were kids, but since puberty we've become vastly different people. He's more convenient than likable.

PETER: Your Snapchats were hilarious. Looks like you had an eventful summer.

PETER and MAX start walking to class.

MAX: I know, I got with like six girls. I'm such a little slut.

PETER stops in his tracks, obviously disturbed by MAX'S comment.

PETER: Dude, that's what annoys me! You're not a slut. And why do the girls get off so easy, why aren't they thought of as sluts? It's like we're shamed for having a sex drive!

MAX: I don't know, it's just different. Come on, we're gonna be late for World History.

PETER ABEL and MAX start rushing off to class.

INT. CLASSROOM—DAYTIME

PETER and MAX sit amongst girls, including the most popular girl in school, boxing superstar HARPER, talking about a back-to-school party.

PETER (V.O.): Harper Sosas. Incredibly skilled at being the worst human to ever walk the earth.

HARPER: I think I want it to be a themed party, something like: CEOs and Secretary Hoes.

MAX: Yeah, and the guys could show up as secretaries—just wearing a tie and boxers.

While all the kids laugh, PETER looks perplexed, but shakes it off and doesn't say anything. Meanwhile, MRS. PLECK, the World History teacher, walks up to the podium and addresses the class.

MRS. PLECK: I assume you all did the summer assignment; so let's jump right in. What did you find most interesting about the early 20th century in Britain?

PETER raises his hand tentatively and MRS. PLECK calls on him.

PETER: I found it fascinating how during the Suffrager's Movement, men began rebelling against society's strict standards of them and demanded the right to vote.

MRS. PLECK: Very true. Now, Peter, why did this interest you so much?

PETER: I guess I just kinda find it relevant to today.

HARPER and kids in the class look at each other. HARPER whispers "meninist" and rolls her eyes mockingly.

HARPER (IN LOUD WHISPER): I just liked reading about how everybody drank so much.

PETER (V.O.): Point in case.

Kids in the class laugh at HARPER's joke. PETER looks uncomfortable and embarrassed that he even spoke at all.

INT. CAR—DAYTIME

PETER and PETER'S DAD sit in the front seat, driving home.

PETER'S DAD: You look like you've had a shit day. Arcade?

PETER looks over at his dad, deflated, but smiles ever so slightly in compliance.

INT. ARCADE—DUSK
Camera pans on several people playing various arcade games, eventually settling on PETER and PETER'S DAD playing air hockey.

PETER: I guess I just feel insecure.

PETER'S DAD: Why, honey?

PETER: I don't think girls like me. At all.

PETER'S DAD: Why would you say that? You're handsome, you're smart . . .

PETER: Dad, you don't get it. I just feel like I'm too opinion-ated or loud or something.

PETER'S DAD: What?

PETER: I don't know. I guess girls like guys who shut up and agree with them. Like I'm a hassle because I believe in things like equality. The girls I know hate that shit. Oh, fuck you, Peter for caring about equal pay? It's so ridiculous. I wish I didn't care, I wish I was like normal guys . . . maybe girls would like me. But also, I claim to be a meninist yet I'm let-ting women's opinions of me define me and my worth. God, it's so confusing.

PETER'S DAD has a sad look in his eyes, but doesn't know how to effectively communicate with his son. He looks down, slightly ashamed and slightly discouraged.

honorsband

ANGELO HERNANDEZ-SIAS, Grade 12, Age 17. Muskegon High
School, Muskegon, MI. Kirk Carlson, *Educator*

Your father's preaching pedestal is the driver's seat. He rests
his hands on the podium and opens his mouth. If you're going
to cheat, he tells you, don't do it in this town. She'll catch you.

You laugh (why do you laugh), his heavy words packed into
one rough brick that skims the top of your scalp, tearing fol-
licles from roots, skin from flesh.

He turns the wheel. The car creaks, rolls over the splitting
asphalt of the Three Oaks parking lot, a collection of side-by-
side driveways that black and brown children utilize to play
Jackpot with foam footballs much like the one your mother's
father taught you to throw six years ago—grip the stitches—
the one with the word *poof* etched into its red underbelly.
None win.

Te quiero mucho, you say, pulling on the door handle, stepping from the car into the air—crisp on your cheeks like dried
tears—and pulling your gray hood over your head. You hop up
two cement steps and knock on Quique's door.

In your head, you ask your father, "Is that why you were a
flight attendant?" No, he tells you. "I love your mother."

Indeed, he lies there too.

"What's with the hole in your wall?" you ask Quique. You know what he will say.

* * *

"My mom pissed me off, that's what happened," he says. You hear his breathing, hard and slow through flared nostrils. You, on the top bunk—his younger brother's bunk—your back resting against the Mexico flag on his wall. Him, on the bottom-bunk, his mouth slightly open now, palms in hair. "What did she do?" you ask him.

"I don't want to talk about it."

* * *

Quique's mom, white and fat, smokes with the windows up—her cigarette in her right hand, the cheetah-print steering wheel slip in her left.

"Mom, when will you quit sucking cancer sticks?" Quique asks.

"When you start minding your own fucking business and quit worrying about grown folks," she says, pressing a little harder on the gas. You rest your head on the window—it jolts.

"I hate it when you say that," he says.

"Emi," she says, her blue eyes cooling yours through the rearview, "tell your friend to watch his mouth before I turn this car around and take both of your asses home."

"I don't want to get involved," you say, smiling (why do you smile).

You know Quique hates it when you smile. You wince when he sees you.

* * *

Beyond the wide cafeteria window is an infinite stretch of pine trees. You and Quique are the golden arches, about a mile away, that protrude from them.

Everyone is white; you are cold. You left your sweater in Quique's room. He, too, is shivering am I the cold's cause or the cause's cold or the cause's cold's cold will I ever be warm I will never be warm enough.

There are silver tables, thirty of them, with black edges. You and Quique land at a table full of boys with white necks. Quique offers his hand. It is not burnt; they do not accept. Both of you sit.

The five of them stand, leave, and sit again—this time, at the table next to yours—and continue their laughing and talking. On the wall at the far side of the room hangs a giant German flag. You and Quique stare.

* * *

"Ask her for her number," Quique says. She, across the room, her toothpick-colored face mostly concealed by her matted hair, brown and flat on her small head. Her eyes, too small to see—Grammy's old diamond earrings.

"I don't mess with white girls," you lie.

"Bullshit," he says. "Why don't you talk to her?"

"I have a girlfriend." How convenient.

"If I didn't, you can bet your ass I'd be up there quicker than you can say, Stop. "

"I'm sure."

"Fine. Don't go. I'll go."

He smiles. Your feet are heavy—pale—in your shoes.

"Hi," you tell her, your voice cracking like a walnut.

"Hey, kid," she tells you. Her eyes, no longer shining. Her friends, beside her, their eyes duller. You are brown, born for the sun—not the clouds. Why "kid," you do not ask her, though the words are nearly bursting from your lips.

"What's your name," you say.

"Why?" she asks you. Quique snorts.

You will kill him for it.

* * *

The clouds have left, but the sky is black. You and Quique, alone, your backs on white wall cement. His right hand taps his torn trumpet case; his left hand's fingertips linger into the gaps of the gray-brown vent on which you sit. A white man approaches you, asks, "Where are your parents?"

"They're almost here," Quique tells him. The man leaves.

"Hey," he starts. His voice, familiar. You've tasted Quique's hey a thousand times before.

"What?" you ask.

A sigh. "Never mind," he says.

"OK," you say.

"I want to tell you something," he says.

"Tell me."

"I can't," he says, his head bent, his fingers straining the sweat from his palm like water from soaked ashes.

"Why not?" you ask.

"It's hard to say. I was . . . it was in first grade."

"Someone . . . touched you?" you ask.

He nods his head.

You are silent. "I'm so . . ."

His mother is here. He grabs his trumpet and you follow him out of the door. His mother asks him, "How was rehearsal?"

He says nothing.

"It was good," you tell her.

* * *

Later, him—passing you your own phone through the slot between the wall and his brother's bunk with words etched into a notepad on the cracked screen:

sucking bottom

i was the woman.

Tonight, you will leave him alone.

TAMRA GOULD, *PANDA*, Grade 12, Age 18, Edmond North
High School, Edmond, OK. Stacy Johnson, *Educator*

What to Wear

KARA HILL, Grade 8, Age 12. Platte City Middle School, Platte City, MO. Kelly Miller, *Educator*

Wear makeup. This is an important event. You want to look re-fined, you want to look nice and sophisticated. But don't wear too much and don't wear it the wrong way. Don't wear the wrong kind, or you'll send the wrong message. First impres-sions are very important. But wait, there are already a million labels pasted to your back because you own a pair of breasts. Don't wear makeup.

Wear a dress. If you want to attract a man, you need to catch his eye. Look nice or you'll never find a good husband. If you don't look good enough, you won't catch his eye, and then where will you be? But don't put too much on display, or you'll be a slut. You have to watch out for the wrong kind of men.

You can never be sure what they'll do, so be careful. If you walk out there like that, they won't be able to control them-selves. Boys will be boys. Don't wear a dress.

Wear jewelry. The bigger, the shinier, the better. The size shows how much he loves you. But not too big, or it'll just be flashy. It needs to be subtle, tasteful. Don't wear jewelry.

Wear pink. Like a big neon sign saying, "Hey look at me! I'm cute!" Put Christmas lights on your screwed-up personality. Do you really want to be Barbie? Fake. Hot pink, fuchsia, scarlet, blush, show your support of breast cancer! Disease. You look like disease and bubblegum-flavored trash. Don't wear pink.

Wear black. Black? Whose funeral are you going to? Emo trash, depressed, the ashy color of the burned house of your ex-boyfriend. Don't wear black. Wear red. Powerful, confident. Don't scare him off! You look like a prostitute, a mistress, red the color of lust. The color of blood. Don't wear red.

Wear yellow. Oh, honey, that gaudy shade? It doesn't go well with your complexion. You'll look like a child prostitute. Don't wear yellow.

Wear blue. Like that little sky-blue sweater dress with the wool turtleneck that feels like a noose. Heading toward certain death in your high-heeled boots. Don't wear blue.

Wear white. What, like some sort of pure virgin? Don't pretend you're not a slut! If it gets wet, it will be completely see-through. Is that what you want? To be a tramp? Don't wear white.

Wear brown. Great, you'll look like the piece of crap that you are. Wear green. You'll look washed-out and sick. Wear purple. What's wrong with purple? Nothing. But don't wear it, society says so.

Wear nothing. Go naked. Get arrested. Get raped. Be shivering and covered in tears and judgment. Wear your emotions. Your heart on your sleeve. But don't speak your opinions. Men don't like a woman who chatters endlessly. Be disgustingly overdramatic and theatrical, let all your problems show and scare off any potential husband.

Stop existing. With all the judgment and expectations of society. Let any cloth float through you without the need to wear it. End all of it. But what will they dress your corpse in for the funeral?

Twins

AMELIA VAN DONSEL, Grade 11, Age 16. Waltham Senior High School, Waltham, MA. Kevin Kearney, *Educator*

Her tiny cheeks go so red at first they looked freshly slapped, and then I see dirt smiles beneath each fingernail, and I shake her and knock the berries from her hands that are stained with sweet blood and I ask if she ate them, did she really eat them, and she shakes her head in a way that's both yes and no and her hair's waving that's like the fuzz on the belly of a golden retriever; and then she starts screaming and crying and sputtering that yes, yes, she did eat them because Lauren dared her to, and she's screaming something high and pure and shining while in the yard there's people gathering that look like statues with beating hearts, and I'm breathing through my teeth for an ambulance while people say, Oh, Jesus, oh, Jesus, word's out there's been some kid who's stuffed berries in her mouth because Lauren dared her to and after a minute they scramble like pigeons for their phones and there's been a call for an ambulance by some well-meaning religious neighbor who runs to her saying, It's okay, Babydoll, and Babydoll's chest and neck go blotchy scarlet like they're cold, eyes roll up wide like giant lightbulbs and blink hard and she's coughing and people are screaming for Mama because where is she and why does she leave her girls out in the yard like that; but then a metal bed folds out like a flat skeleton from the car that's spinning red and blue and a black man straps her on and says to us but mostly her, It's OK, it's OK, gonna be at the hospital in two minutes flat, because she's choking now, her little plastic cup over her face just like mine going white then clear and a voice that's breaking into pieces behind those big lips while I hold her hand the color of bone and can feel her heart pound like a clock, practically hear it open and close and squeeze itself like the small fists of sleeping children; and then we're rushing through the air that feels like it's ninety-five degrees and humid, clouds dirty as towels; and she's stopped crying because she can hardly breathe now, just rattling and jerking with that cart, and she's pushed ahead of me while I trail after her inside like a pair of broken wings, and more people come up to me asking me things that I don't know I just don't know I just know that I'm screaming for her now while she's thrown behind a flimsy white curtain, more people staring at my face like they've never seen anything so terrible, more people staring, drooped over in waiting-room chairs like dying wisteria; and then doctors pass me and shake me, too, ones with airy-floating white hair and rocky lines of teeth, yanking my arms as I cry and my tiny cheeks go so red they look freshly slapped, and they shake me, my hair that's like the fuzz on the belly of a golden retriever, in a way that's both yes and no, and then I keep screaming and crying and sputtering that yes, yes, she did eat them because I dared her to.

Online Safety, or Overprotection?: Exploring Schools' Rights to Filter Internet Access vs. Students' Rights to Information

MINA YUAN, Grade 11, Age 16. Wayzata High School, Plymouth MN.
Miles Trump, *Educator*

Chicken breast. Sex education. Cello fingering.

None of these phrases are inherently harmful or offensive, yet all of these Internet search terms are blocked on school-issued iPads in the Wayzata Public Schools district. The reason? The phrases contain the terms "breast," "sex," or "fingering," all words deemed inappropriate by the school district's filtering software.

Some students argue that the filter causing these blocks on school technology violates their constitutional rights to receive and express information and limits their education. On the other hand, school administrators say the filter protects students from offensive material and emphasize the district's right to control its own technology.

"The iPads are the property of the school district. Having the very limited scope of educational purpose . . . the district has the ability to set the parameters of use," said Wade Phillips, director of technology at Wayzata. "If there's a violation of these rules . . . there could be consequences."

Controversy Goes Viral at Wayzata

In December, Wayzata junior Nathan Ringo posted an account of his protests of the district's iPad regulations, as well as the response of school administrators, on BoingBoing, a popular online magazine. The conflict began, according to Ringo, when he found a way to evade the school's censorware his sophomore year, and it continued into his junior year.

Ringo wrote that, in response, administrators accused him of cracking the firewall and revoked his Internet access, forcing him to rely on his personal laptop and Internet hotspot in class ever since.

"I can see how a 'better-safe-than-sorry' approach could seem attractive to school administration," Ringo said. "However, I disagree with the logic in this approach—free speech and freedom of the press are essential to education."

Yet, according to Phillips, who couldn't speak directly about Ringo's situation because of data privacy laws, even an administrator's suspicion of a student hacking the district's network, which is potentially harmful to the entire school, provides reason enough for administrators to examine an iPad's contents or to take away Internet access. "That's our obligation as stewards of the school, to protect the privacy of the organization," Phillips said. "Hacking and attacking on the network where they're using it to try to infiltrate or access confidential, secure information . . . We'd have to go investigate that to the full measure of our ability."

Comments on Ringo's article, which went viral internationally, ranged from agreeing with Ringo and comparing school limitations to prison regulations, to reminding him that the district's filters are meant to protect rather than suffocate. Others approved of Ringo's message, but not his method.

"He's doing the right thing, but he's going about it the wrong way," said Pranav Maddula, a Wayzata sophomore who interns at Google. "He's antagonizing the school, (and) he's antagonizing the principal and the tech department. He's getting the word out there, and he's trying to cause change, but . . . the way he's doing it, he's not getting parents or other students to work with him.

Ringo said his article, while unexpectedly widely discussed, did not achieve his original goal, which was a repeal or rewrite of the Children's Internet Protection Act (CIPA). Under the CIPA, schools are allowed E-rate federal funding if they filter all potentially offensive images from student access. As a recipient of E-rate funding, Wayzata follows the CIPA. "There is no mention of blocking entire web pages in the CIPA," Ringo said. "The current censorship at Wayzata blocks a lot more material than the ruling provides for."

However, administrators say that even without E-rate funding, the district is morally obligated to filter any objectionable material, including web pages, to protect its students.

Safety vs. Overprotection

Administrators in no way purposefully keep useful material from students, according to Mike Dronen, director of technology at Minnetonka Public Schools. Instead, they strive to shelter students from content such as hate speech, pornography, and gambling.

"I don't think there's really any stepping on constitutional rights by providing a web filter, but I think there could be an argument made that not providing a web filter could be some form of disservice to students," Dronen said. "If a student could click on anything at anytime and have any form of content in a school environment, where there could be a web filter, that definitely would not be good either."

Maddula agreed with the need for a filter at Wayzata, but argued that some systems can be overprotective.

"It's very progressive, but it blocks way too much to be counted as useful," he said. "It's almost like [administrators] are imposing guidelines on what they think we should be doing with our time and with our technology instead of letting us do what's actually useful."

Maddula's personal connection to the filter has only reinforced his opinions of the system. After spending the last two years reviewing code as an intern for Google at its headquarters in California, Maddula used his programming experience and strong opinions to help Wayzata administrators review the filter system as iPads first arrived at the high school.

"We talked a lot about how we could improve the experience," Maddula said. "I did the initial block list, and I checked over the blocks to make sure nothing accidentally got blocked . . . The old [system] used to be just a list of websites that the school deemed not beneficial for learning, or not proper for school . . . Now they're blocking a lot based on keywords in the URL or in the website. I suggest toning it down a bit."

Phillips said problems such as excessive blocking arise because the filter works as a database with different categories, such as "obscene" or "harmful to minors." Depending on its category, a website is either blocked or allowed on school technology.

"Filtering the Internet is a very complicated and difficult situation," he said. "You can't just categorize everything, and I think that's one of the limitations of having a filter. It just doesn't fall into a black-and-white scenario."

While keywords may trigger the filter to categorize certain websites incorrectly, Phillips emphasized that it was not administrators' goal or intent to do so, and that speaking to teachers and administrators to get such sites unblocked would be the best response for students.

District's Constitutional Rights vs. Students' Rights

According to attorney and University of St. Thomas media law professor Mark Anfinson, schools have the right to filter, but he thinks "it's a pretty dicey proposition for school administrations to censor or block students [from] accessing certain websites," he said.

"It's much less justifiable for them to do that than to prohibit a bad message that the student is expressing," Anfinson said. "How do you know as a school administrator [that] simply visiting a particular website, how can you know that's going to have some terrible adverse effect on people? You can't."

The First Amendment rights of public high school students, while weaker than those of public college students, still hold considerable weight, Anfinson said. He noted that the Supreme Court has defined the First Amendment to include the right to receive information as well as to speak it, even for public high school students.

He also likened the iPad conflict at Wayzata to the debate over the censorship of books in school libraries in the late 1900s, in which school boards would ban literature for containing sexual references or curse words. According to Anfinson, nearly every time a book was banned, the school would get sued for violating the First Amendment—and it would lose.

As for schools' argument that iPads are their own property, Anfinson pointed out that the book censorship debate serves as precedent.

"I don't think the fact that it's the school's iPad allows them to curtail your First Amendment rights in any way, shape, or form," Anfinson said. "To my knowledge, no court ever said that because they're the school's books, that gave them the stronger right to censor. That would never fly . . . They can't censor [iPads] without very strong justification. However, the legal opinion on censorship and surveillance depends hugely on varying circumstances in different schools.

"First Amendment communication law is very much like a kaleidoscope," said Anfinson. "A slight change in the facts you have to deal with changes the legal analysis."

Opening Up the Conversation

In some cases, certain sites are requested to be blocked by students. When Dronen worked at Stillwater Area Public Schools, Facebook was blocked on school technology because the student council was concerned students would be distracted by social media, he said.

"I think there's always going to be some conversation back and forth, and I think as long as students can be having conversations with teachers or building or district leaders . . . everyone gets to move forward," Dronen said. "There may be things that students don't understand, and there are definitely things teachers and administrators don't understand. To hear that student voice and listen to it can be really helpful."

To encourage that conversation, Dronen suggested schools establish a student technology group, such as the Tech Mates, which are Minnetonka student groups that meet regularly with administrators at both the middle school and high school to discuss issues with school-issued iPads. Another opportunity for student-administrator communication lies in broadcasts such as "Beyond 140," a video that airs at Minnetonka High School every month to address the characteristics of proper technology use and digital citizenship, Dronen said. At Wayzata, there is no technological student group like Tech Mates, according to Phillips.

"That may be something we can improve on in the future," Phillips said. "If there is further opportunity for dialogue, whether it's organized or unorganized, from a student perspective, on what we can do to help you get what you need to succeed in your life, that would be our goal."

While debate exists surrounding school filters and surveillance, both administrators and students agree that improved communication is the most likely solution.

"This is going to continue to percolate," Anfinson said. "Nathan Ringo is not the only Nathan Ringo out there. What is needed and would be most valuable is a little better of an opportunity for students and administration to communicate."

One in Eight Million

SADIE COWLES, Grade 8, Age 13. Frank H. Harrison Middle School, Yarmouth, ME. Charlotte Agell, *Educator*

It was obvious from the curious glances and the blatant stares that Nanchi Village, with its population of 600 people, was not used to getting visitors, let alone visitors from America. It also didn't help that we had the "mayor" of the village, Mr. Shen, leading us around on his scooter. My family and I were on a trip in China for the first time since my brother and I were adopted over ten years ago. The trip back was a long-awaited event for our whole family. We planned to visit six different cities, which included orphanage tours and visits to our "finding places," where we had been left by our birth parents. I had also made the decision to seek out my birth parents, even though the odds of finding them in a country with so many people were extremely unlikely, like finding a single grain of rice in a vast rice paddy.

The visit to my finding place was very different than any of us thought it would be. The city where I am from, Zhanjiang, has a population of 8 million people. However, once we arrived in Zhanjiang, Yaoyao, our Chinese exchange student (who was traveling with us), translated the police report that told us where I was found. We were all extremely surprised! We learned that I was actually from an island in Zhanjiang called Hai Dao in a small rural village named Nanchi. This was an immense shock since I had grown up thinking that I was from a huge city, making the finding of my birth parents nearly impossible. Now, the odds of finding my birth parents had gone up considerably. We met Mr. Shen, the leader of my village, after finding his number listed on a sign in front of the Community Center. Yaoyao called him on a cell phone and he showed up minutes later in a straw hat and worn clothes, riding a scooter. We told Mr. Shen that I was trying to find my birth parents and that we had made posters that I intended to put up around the village. He was very understanding about our situation and asked us if we would like his help. We said yes, of course, but he insisted that he take us out to lunch first.

This was unlike any eating experience in America; the meal included pig tongue, which tasted similar to beef, but tougher. We selected our food from buckets with live crustaceans, rather than from a menu. Throughout our trip I learned that you cannot judge a restaurant's food by how it looks from the outside. Some of the restaurants we ate at, including the one in Nanchi, looked slightly unrefined, but when the food came out it was delicious.

After looking at the small 9x12-inch posters my parents and I had carefully constructed, Mr. Shen shook his head and told Yaoyao that we needed to get bright-red paper to make the posters more visible. We followed him in the minivan we had rented for the day, and he quickly stopped at a store and went inside. He reappeared with big sheets of China-red paper and a container of thick sticky glue and a brush. We lay the sheets of paper on the ground, holding them down with rocks and proceeded to glue my posters to the paper. We tried to let them-dry, but Mr. Shen quickly hopped back up on his scooter and motioned for us to follow.

* * *

In China they refer to people by their family name, which in my village is Shen. Most families live within the same village, so they all have the same last name. If I had stayed in Nanchi, then I would most likely have been a Shen as well. Mr. Shen had dark-tan skin from working outside on his fish farm. He wore a wide-brimmed straw hat like most men in the village, and was probably in his early 60's. He had many wrinkles where his eyebrows furrowed when he squinted. He was dressed in a simple outfit of long pants, flip-flops, and a short-sleeved button-down shirt, over which he wore a jacket, which seemed ridiculous to us, considering south China's hot humid air. Mr. Shen, like many others we saw in China, was missing a few middle top and bottom teeth, which unnerved me for a period of time, but throughout the day I got used to it.

Once the posters were ready, we all piled into the van and followed Mr. Shen on his scooter. He stopped at the corner of a building and we all climbed out. I handed him one of the posters, he slathered on some glue and plastered it onto the side of the building. As we were putting the poster up, people dressed similarly to Mr. Shen in simple pants, hats, and button-down shirts started coming out of their houses and apartments and leaving their market stalls to come and see what the commotion was. They all chattered excitedly in Chinese, which at the beginning of our journey had sounded to us like arguing. Some of them pointed at me, explaining the situation to those just joining. Throughout this whole trip we had been stared at unabashedly like we were exotic animals in town for the day. I did not like all of the attention and felt a bit uncomfortable. If I had stayed in this village, I probably would have known all of these people. In a village this small I guessed that everyone knew each other. At another stop we put a poster up, and then got back in the car to wait for Mr. Shen to return. We sat in the van and watched people come over in groups and look at the poster. They started gesturing toward the van so Yaoyao rolled down the windows. They peered in and looked at the strange American family, my mom and sister with their blonde hair, my tall father with his head almost touching the roof of the car, and then Zhi and I, the Chinese adoptees with the foreign American family.

As we continued down the dirt roads like a mini-parade of people to the four different entrances to the town, we saw shops that were overflowing with plastic chairs, hats, brooms, plastic bins, fans, baskets, and all sorts of odds and ends. There were stands with watermelons and baskets of shan zhù, a dark-purple and messy fruit we had come to love. The most common sight was umbrellas, everyone had one covering them and their produce. Most Chinese try to avoid the sun, as their idea of beauty is to have very fair skin. As we walked around China everywhere you looked, people were carrying parasols.

It was hard to picture myself living in such a small village. Looking down the main street at the aging apartment buildings and the fairly unoccupied market, there didn't seem to be much happening. I would most likely have been uneducated, and when I got older I would work in a factory in a nearby city. I would also have spoken Chinese, not English. At the time I was adopted, the Chinese government's policy allowed each family to have only one child, but if both parents were only children, they could have two children. This rule is more heavily enforced in the city than in the countryside, so I most likely would have had multiple brothers and sisters. My family would likely be poor, I would not have much, and I certainly would never have gotten the chance to go to America. Similarly, I would not have any of the opportunities that I have now. This is supposed to make me feel lucky, but to be honest, I would not have known what I was missing. Is it all about having the most opportunities? Just because I lived in a different place does not mean that I wouldn't be as content and loved by my family and friends in China as I am now in America. I would be a similar person, but I believe the setting you grow up in and who you are surrounded by does have a big impact on the person you become.

We continued putting up posters. Each poster had two baby pictures of me and last year's school picture. We included information about where I was left, when I was born, and an agreement to keep all information confidential. After each poster went up, people assembled and started reading them. We guessed that by the end of the day, almost everyone in that village had seen the posters. The odds were looking good for finding my birth parents, but I was trying to keep from being too optimistic so that I wouldn't be let down. We were not sure how long the posters would last before wear and tear and wind and rain tore them down. Who knew if we would even get a call or if someone would step forward? We would just have to wait and see.

Six months later, after several calls and one DNA test, it was determined that my birth parents had not been found. I remember telling someone that if the DNA test wasn't positive that it would be devastating, but it wasn't. I was disappointed and upset that the situation had not turned out the way I wanted it to. I was also slightly relieved because the potential father had been very sick. Meeting him might have been difficult because most people in China do not have access to affordable health care. He also might have had a genetic disease that could have been passed on to me.

We had known the whole time that the odds of finding birth parents were very slim in such a big country. I'm guessing that all of the people in my village and surrounding villages have seen my posters or heard about them by now. Hopefully someone will still step forward. Maybe they are worried that they will get in trouble for abandoning a child or for having more children than was allowed at the time. It's also possible they moved, or maybe they even died. Regardless, I was able to hear two families' stories, so I have a much clearer picture of what my story may have been. Even if nothing more happens, I have had a glimpse of how my life might have turned out had I grown up in a small village on the other side of the world, in China.

The Mothers

KATHERINE DU, Grade 11, Age 15. Greenwich Academy, Greenwich, CT.
Jeff Schwartz, *Educator*

My grandmother is eight years old when she sees her birth mother's ovaries bleed into a wooden bucket. She hears moaning. Melting. Something godless as the blood pours like congealed tea from a flask.

Forty hours later, the light unfastens tenderly from her birth mother's eyes.

* * *

Months after her birth, my grandmother is sold to a family with food and a stillborn daughter. They live on the other side of the mountains, away from Chongqing, away from the war. They will love a ghost. Clothe her. Feed her. She will swipe scraps in the dark, find a way to send them back to her five blood siblings.

The family with food is a textile tycoon. It yawns, rich from the blood of others. Before her eyes know to lower, her voice to cool, my grandmother asks where the lily-like puffs are born. Her milk mother holds her like a glass doll. Cotton is a dream, my angel. Never question the mother of dreams.

It is December 13, 1937, a day as timeworn as bloodless winter light. My grandmother is beginning to forget the shape of her birth mother's voice when they descend: the Japanese, their gun-licked fingers, their salt-smoked lips.

Three hundred thousand Chinese will sprinkle these streets. Unborn children glued to the tips of bayonets. Bodies in the dust. Most are women with bellies sliced open like flayed salmon, purple-bruised legs splayed out in invitation.

* * *

My grandmother's milk mother leaves her textile factory in Jiangsu hours before the Rape of Nanjing, only to die weeks later of the influenza. My grandmother will call it the miracle that knifed her in the heart. A swollen dream.

* * *

At seven years old, my grandmother leaves the empty house of textiles. With a cotton bag of prayers and morsels, she walks three hundred li through the remains of the Sichuan countryside. One hundred miles through a world of feral fear. All around her are volcanoes of upturned dirt, frosted shells of peasants, broken faith. Sometimes she kisses her hands to the dusty fields so her tears can sting the earth.

After two suns and moons pass, a mountain ridge creeps toward her with no beginning or end. She sees a dip down the middle, a gorgeous wound. A memory surfaces: her milk mother's warning. Bandits roam the place where the mountain sinks.

But the pangs of hunger cut her, devour her, become her. Her bamboo sandals carve rivers of blood on the soles of her feet as she runs. Ascends. Presses on. Dusk swallows the luster of the day. She persists. Sweat licks her cotton bag, the spaces where her face meets hair. Her eyes shudder, but she forces them open. Pretends they are orbs of fire. Soon the sun drips scarlet blood on the canvas of the sky.

* * *

A year after my grandmother returns to her homeland, her birth mother bleeds endlessly. My grandmother learns to pack, then unpack, a box of ice around her heart.

Allows an ugly hunger to become the pulse of her life.

Eventually her eldest sister embraces Chairman Mao, and the five blood siblings are fed well and taught the ways of the world. They spring fire from wet matches. Attend Chongqing University. The Japanese exchange students and professors inflame my grandmother at first, but on a fateful day of downpour, she slips in a pool of mud. A tender hand stretches before her eyes. She holds it. She will never let go of the Japanese professor who shows her that a nation does not define its people, that forgiveness is the only weapon that can end war.

* * *

In 1967, my grandmother flees a Chongqing ruptured by opposition factions within Chairman Mao's paramilitary. Eight One Five captures the northern bank of the Jialing River, while Opposition Until Death sticks guns through the southern cherry laurels of Chongqing University. My grandmother wraps her daughter in her arms. Scales the mountain behind the university. Eight One Five's bullets sail toward their fading bodies. She is breathless. Boneless. Pockets of earth erupt inches away. In her mind, she is again on the mountain of her youth. That gorgeous wound. She is drinking the story of her blood, cresting the mountain to the place where the sun will rise.

Sausages

KATIE MLINEK, Grade 11, Age 16. George Washington Carver Center for Arts and Technology, Towson, MD. Suzanne Supplee, *Educator*

Marie creaked my bedroom door open, the closest to a hello that I would get, and stood with her back turned to me. I could hear her trying to control her breathing.

"Marie!" I gave my best I've-been-doing-my-homework-for-hours look, complete with spastic eye movements and un-brushed hair. "How are you doing, dear?" She turned to face me, and I could see glints of tear trails down her face. Melodrama bubbled beneath all the gasps she took of air, as if she had just been sobbing in her room, alone, in the dark (she's fond of that last touch—darkness).

"Did you eat the sausages?" she asked me. "Um, no," I said. "What sausages?"

"The ones from yesterday. Did. You. Eat. Them."

I shook my head again and she slammed my door shut behind her with an overly loud, "UGH!" I threw aside the stacks of chemistry problems I had been working on, glad for an excuse to procrastinate, and crept from my room to the top of the staircase. I could hear pots and pans clattering against each other with more emphasis than usual. As I walked down the stairs, the wails from my sisters grew louder.

"What is going on?" I asked, stepping into the kitchen.

"Someone threw away the sausages," my mom said.

"What sausages? Why is everyone talking about sausages? This is ridiculous." My sisters looked up at me, rubbing their wet faces, squinting like they'd been blinded by the light of Jesus.

"It is not ridiculous." My mom's voice was lower now, my cue to stop preaching my wisdom. "Someone threw away the sausages—or ate them—when I specifically said not to. Specifically. I said, specifically, to keep them."

"Well, I wash the pots and pans after dinner," I said and glanced over at the stack ready for me today. The pile spilled from the sink and onto the counter. "I don't deal with sausages. This isn't my problem."

Immediately, my sisters began defending themselves.

"I didn't even eat one of the sausages," Lizzie said.

"Me too, me too, I didn't even eat dinner yesterday!" Rose said.

A car door shut outside and everyone craned their heads to see through the front door.

My mom rubbed her forehead. "Girls, please stop crying and put the dishes on the table," she said. Rose let out a sob. "Do it silently," my mom added. The door opened and my dad came through.

"How was everyone's day?" he asked. They glanced at him before quickly looking away, no one able to bring themselves to a response. "Oh," he said, "one of those days." My mom led him into their room and shut the door. As my sisters finished setting the table in silence, I kept tabs on my parents' bedroom. The longer the door was shut, the angrier my mom was. It was shut for a long time.

At the dinner table that night, no one talked. We passed around the warmed-up mac-n-cheese, the sort that was sticky and didn't taste cheesy at all, with fleeting eye contact and only slight chair shuffling. My dad cleared his throat, enough to make Anna whimper and Marie tear up. He began.

"I work very hard every day for you girls," he said. We all knew he wouldn't raise his voice, which was even worse than a short yelling session. He talked to us like one of his business partners. We knew who the boss was. "When I spend all day working for you guys, I'd like to come home and eat the sausages that I bought. But no. Mom says someone threw the leftovers away or ate them. I don't care which it was. What I do know is that they're gone. My sausages, that I bought, are gone."

More howls. Even Miriam, too young to understand the serious situation at hand, began to cry. My dad stood up from the table and walked downstairs, not bothering pushing in his chair. Marie screamed how sorry she was, how she was probably the one who threw away the sausages, how, heck, she couldn't even remember there being any sausages.

"Today," my mom said, "you should throw the leftovers away."

Normally, we listen to music and sing while cleaning, but on this night, the night of the sausages, we only focused on the leftovers. I stood in front of the sink, not sure where to even begin. Rose trembled as she swept the floor, Lizzie wiped off the counter while choking back tears, and Anna sat curled up in the corner. Marie stared at the trash as if looking for last night's sausages, not quite ready to throw away the food on her plate.

Skins

RYAN ZUBERY, Grade 12, Age 17. Capital High School, Boise, ID.
Paula Uriarte, *Educator*

I—Dirt

Dirt, they called me. Chocolate on a good day, shit-face on a
bad one, but we'd always come back to dirt. It was a nice catch-
all—dirt captured my baseness, my uncleanliness, and the
strong likelihood that worms and ants and multilegged things
lurked just beneath my surface.

"Run!" they'd shout in terror. "Don't let dirt touch you or
else you'll have to shower!" Tag suddenly became more frantic
when I was involved. It was no longer a game but a threat.
Should I outstretch a grasping, dark hand to capture a dove, I'd
have committed a grave crime: to tarnish that which is pure.
Most days, their thin legs, hewn from frigid marble, would carry them safely away from me, and they'd maintain a distance
to ensure their survival.

She let down her guard, though. The hunt was over as we
filed into the classroom, but that didn't stay my hand from
clasping on to her exposed shoulder, meeting her skin with
mine. "Gotcha," I whispered with a grin, completely unaware
of what I had done. The brazen act wasn't lost on her, how-

ever; her head of fire burned ardently and her eyes of sapphire drowned themselves. "What did you do?" she lamented. But it could not be undone. She was marked henceforth, my hand leaving the impression of a soiled boot in a bed of fresh snow.

My classmates were certainly in possession of a great amount of ingenuity, as before long, they'd devised a caste system, and I was the untouchable. Or perhaps I give them too much credit and such a hierarchy is self-evident. Either way, I was at the bottom, but it didn't matter because she was now down there with me. A friend! Dirt's girlfriend, they started to call her, a phrase that would set off a feeling akin to anxiousness, but nicer somehow.

She too sat alone now at lunch! It never occurred to me that such a downgrade would cause her to resent me—I just saw it as an opportunity to have lunch with someone else for once and maybe, if I was lucky, that nice anxious feeling would return. So, I situated myself at her table and got out my lunch sack. At that moment, she became flushed out of the disgrace she had to bear. "What are you doing here?" she questioned, to which I just smiled and replied that I thought we could talk and eat lunch together. With the eyes of the rest of the class focused in on her, she curtly responded with her opinion of me, gathered up her food, and left for another table.

Disgusting. That's what she called me.

Soap was soon in short supply. Hot water never seemed to be available. Nonetheless, I sat over the sink every day, hand caressing hand in a scalding froth. But it wouldn't wash away. For half an hour each day, I'd sit in the shower, scrubbing every patch of my being, but it wouldn't come off.

But the dreams! There, there was always solace. Thirty minutes after crawling into bed beside my parents, I could cast off my dark prison and be reborn as a fair one. There, I could be one of them, with fine porcelain skin and eyes that gleamed in the dark. There, I could be beautiful, a winter child molded from snowflakes, fragile and arrogant. There, I could be pure, a blank sheet without blemishes or stains. There, I could sit with her and hold her hand.

But the dreams would end in blurred eyes and a return to the dark room about me.

II—Disease

When the blight came, I cannot recall; it may have been with a fever, on my tenth birthday, or perhaps I'd just never paid it attention. They said that it was likely my inheritance or the result of chance, but I knew it was the answer that proved God, in fact, was listening and had a twisted sense of humor.

My standing with the others didn't change but was only given a fresh coat of paint. Whereas before, my isolation was attributed to maintaining a social order, now it was a quarantine made in an abundance of caution, in case my condition was transferable. When I was spoken to, it was to be asked, "What's that on your face?"

That's when the façade came up, when various creams and powders were applied to my face, when covering up was compulsory, when my bangs were grown out and conveniently swept to the right. Yet I was exposed to all that would notice through treatment; ointments rendered my face oily, and Sunday mornings were spent in the courtyard, reclining in a lawn chair with nothing on but a pair of underwear, skin fully exposed to the sun and passersby.

But nevermind the abuses of my classmates or the furtive glances of the neighbors. The biggest concern was my relatives.

The lush, verdant fields and swamplands that sit beneath the high red sun felt no more a home than the purple mountains

I left behind. The sway of my speech was different, colloqui-alisms couldn't flow from my mouth unimpeded. The stan-dard greeting I received every couple of years once I got off the plane was the same: *"Arre, bhai,* you're still not fair after living in America for so long?" It was, after all, the national obsession; I lost track of how many different billboards adver-tised skin-bleaching products on the way home. Through the window, I caught a quick glimpse of some of the gorib on the streets. One shielded her face from the sun, bunching up her shari like a niqab, to hide a splash of white that disfigured her face. I suppose I wasn't the only one who whispered their de-sires to the universe while they fell asleep, hoping that some-one would hear them.

We stayed at my cousin's house, as we always did, but I was well aware it wasn't my home. I couldn't run around, bare-footed, with reckless abandon any longer, nor wear shorts that exposed my kneecaps. Socks and long pants were my burka, but without any sense of purpose in wearing them, as they'd simply collect the dust and dirt on the floor. Before any vis-it by more distant relatives, I'd be whisked off to the vanity, where I'd apply makeup to my upper brow against my sense of pride, a layer of soil meant to disguise the sickly permafrost. It was done to keep me safe, to shield me from the callous words that fell with no great difficulty nor shame from my relatives' mouths. Before every encounter, I drilled the set responses to their queries about my condition should the makeup smear and expose me. The disease had hardened my skin, but it had an internal toll. I prepared in naught, spent my hours in vain for the question that never came, and all I had to show for it were deeper wounds I formed by picking at them. My more distant relatives contented themselves with a pinch of the cheek and a "mashallah" before they paid me no more attention.

By custom, they came late and stayed later, so we children were shooed off to bed while the adults' raucous conversation carried on. My cousin and I slipped into bed, but we weren't content to go to sleep without having a late-night conversation of our own. Under the mosquito netting that had always made me feel safe, a third-world canopy, we talked about whatever came up, about school and superheroes, about girls while I simultaneously, but silently, thought about boys, about our futures when one day he too would move to America. But, just before he drifted off, he spoke in a soft voice and asked, "Bhaia, have you ever dreamed what it'd be like to be white?"

I turned away from my cousin and rubbed off my makeup onto the cool pillow, leaving streaks of brown powder against the otherwise clean, light linen. "No," I replied with complete composure before closing my eyes to the dimly lit room and its mosquito netting. "Why would anyone do that?"

III—Blood & Scars

By the time I was a teenager, I'd learned to keep my head down to avoid the stares of others. Exposure didn't have a good history with me, so I endeavored to keep a low-key profile. In spite of keeping a meticulous hygiene regiment, a remnant of earlier years, that defining teenage experience became known to me.

Soon, the gently sloping planes of my face saw the earth crack and rupture, twisting up to form volcanoes that wept ceaselessly and bled lava over the land without reason. In their wake, they left a desolation of fires, burnt earth, and great, blackened calderas imprinting great scars and clefts in the landscape, ensuring that their memory never be forgotten.

Long gone was the desire for a picturesque landscape blanketed in snow. In its stead, I yearned for the ancestral lands that I'd spurned, that perhaps were never mine: the rich, fertile soil baked beneath the high sun that teemed with vitality, the soil that was the lifeblood and pride of all that lived there. Dreams now all focused on that lost ideal.

School, for all the years that had passed, remained largely the same, but I'd learned that it'd be easier if I was the evasive one. Don't make eye contact, and then others have less time to focus in on the flaws of my complexion, for there was always ample material there for critique; my face was a motley tapestry, woven of brown skin and white skin and red skin and black skin.

Yet others were so close. Their hands hung there, limply by their sides, and all I'd have to do was reach out to hold one. I couldn't quite recall when was the last time I had held someone else's hand, interlacing my fingers between theirs. It didn't matter to me if it was a masculine or feminine one—I just wanted to know again what it felt like. Were they warm and soft and comforting or cold and calloused and reassuring, or something in between?

At night, I lay alone in my bed and attempted to clear my head of thoughts, but those of the past kept creeping back in without welcome from the subzero blizzard raging outside. They raced around my mind, punctuated by warm exhalations as I drew my legs closer to my chest, arms grasping shoulders to stave off the cold, my skin completely pressed up against itself in an embrace.

"____," I whispered softly as I rocked gently back and forth in that dark room. "Wasn't that her name?"

The Floppy Arm

PEYTON VASQUEZ, Grade 8, Age 13. Bonnette Junior High School, Deer Park, TX. Veronica Serna, *Educator*

Well, if cancer wasn't bad enough, now my arm won't work. I just learned how to walk down stairs again, which was really hard when my feet would barely come off the floor before they dropped again. Neuropathy is the fancy word the oncologist called my diagnosis when I couldn't run, descend stairs and ramps, tie my shoes, pick up coins, or even button my pants. Even if I tried to hold the rail right now to get down the steps to run away before anyone noticed, it would be impossible because my arm is completely dead.

I'm trying to play Minute to Win It. It's this game my family is playing with some friends where we have to do these tricks where I need both arms to work. It doesn't matter how hard I try to move the tissues that I'm supposed to blow with a straw, my arm just will not work. FLOP! It falls on the table instead of holding the straw. I cannot hold it, but I try and try and try with no success. My arm just keeps flopping. Flop. Flop. Flop. We lose. Because my arm is making this flopping noise when it falls on the table, people are starting to stare and ask questions, especially my mom.

The people we are playing with are a part of my club. It's a club no one wants to belong to because it is only for kids with cancer, not like a real organization where kids choose to sign up like chess club. In fact, it's not really a club at all, but a group of people who get together because of the unfortunate circumstance that my friends and me have or have had cancer. I joined this club when I was diagnosed with stage IIB, intermediate risk, parameningeal embryonal rhabdomyosarcoma. Rhabdo for short. The kids at this get-together are cancer patients or siblings of cancer patients. We meet like this so that we all feel normal. Some of the kids don't have eyes. Some are bald. Some don't have legs. One of us is in a wheelchair. I have to wear tinted protective lenses at all times. That's right. I wear sunglasses at night. But here that's normal and no one stares or asks annoying questions.

All the parents of cancer patients are worriers. Every little cough is a big deal because well, it could really be cancer that has metastasized. I know I have to hide this arm thing because pretty soon all the moms will come to my rescue and annoy me by being overbearingly caring. Most kids probably want their parents to care about them when they are sick, but I have had my fair share. I'd just like to be a normal kid, and actually, I'd just like to be able to win Minute to Win It.

I try to come up with a plan. I fail. The interrogations from my mom begin: "What is going on with your arm?" "Why is your arm twitching?" "Can you raise your hand?" I tell her I'm OK, but I know her. She isn't going to let this go. I just try to make my arm work. Come on, Arm. Come on, Brain.

While heading home, I think I have somewhat gotten away with this arm thing because no one else asked what was going on the rest of the weekend. I keep my hand in my pocket to hide that my arm just will not work. It's lifeless, with the exception of the constant twitching like a fish out of the water trying to make its way back in.

When I go to school Monday, I really think that I fooled everyone and make a break for it. But I have this teacher, the kind that notices my arm right away and starts asking questions and doesn't hesitate to call my mom. The bad part: She calls from the classroom where everyone can hear. That's when I find out that I have a doctor's appointment. My stomach sinks down to my feet that don't work well either. All I do is go to the doctor. After I was diagnosed with cancer last year, had chemo for 42 weeks and radiation for 6 weeks, I have had enough of doctors. If I ever see another doctor, it will be too soon. I know I have to go though. Again. More doctors.

Although Mom and I walk into Dr. Segura's office, I feel pretty good about this. Dr. Segura is a regular doctor. He is the doctor who took care of me before cancer. He only knows me as Peyton and treats me like a regular kid. I've only seen him once since my cancer treatment was over because I was sick. The regular kind of sick. The kind of sick that regular kids get. It felt good to be regular sick. Weird.

I can't climb on the exam table because my arm doesn't work, so my mom has to lift me. I don't like this because I am eight and can climb by myself. Only I can't. I try to tell my arm to stop twitching and start working, but it won't. Dr. Segura comes in and does a bunch of testing. He pushes my legs and makes me point my toes. I think he has lost his mind. I'm not there for my legs. My arm won't work. Then, he makes me shrug my shoulders. The right shoulder moves, but the left does not. It just won't move. No matter how hard I try. It just won't move. It twitches. Just twitches. .

Dr. Segura is concerned. He says I need to go back to Texas Children's Hospital. The good news is that I don't have to go until the next week. I will be better in a couple of days. I just know. I'll be sure of it.

All that changes the next day after school when I'm at the shoe store. I look up and smile at my mom after I find a pair of shoes that I really like. She freaks out and starts telling me to smile with both sides of my face. I smile as big as I can. She grabs her phone from her purse and dials the cancer center. Now I know I'm in big trouble. My mom can't get in touch with our regular nurse, so she dials the afterhours emergency number and starts wildly talking and crying and shouting at me to smile and telling me that if I'm kidding I better knock it off, but I seriously have no idea why she has lost all control. She was completely irrational. We rush to Texas Children's Emergency Room because the doctor thinks I've had a stroke, because when I smile, only one side of my face moves. Great. Just great. More things that don't work.

When we get to the hospital, I get hooked up to all kinds of monitors and IVs. The doctors check out my brain. It was still there and functioning, but didn't show signs of a stroke, so I had to have a total body neurological MRI. It took what seemed like forever, but really it was two hours. The doctors couldn't find a cause for all my symptoms. In their infinite wisdom, they diagnose me with depression. The doctors explain that it's normal for kids with cancer to get depressed and have psychosomatic symptoms. Strange thing is that I am the happiest person alive because I beat a very rare and deadly form of cancer.

It was a hard time for me and my family. My arm would dangle limply at my side for months. I had to go to talking therapy because my parents believed I was depressed as well as physical and occupational therapy. It was really difficult to try to tie my shoes when only one hand worked. In therapy, I had to do all kinds of things like climb stairs, pick up coins, write with my left hand, and touch my fingers to my thumb, which frustrated me because these things were easy before cancer. All this happened until we went to a soccer game one day.

My family sat in a really great suite with a terrific view and our very own waiter. The best part was that there was this short wall dividing our side of the suite from the others. I kept jumping over it. My good arm would swing when I ran to leap over that hurdle, but my left arm would just flop next to my ribs. Mom was getting pretty mad and told me not to jump anymore. I kept jumping. She told me that if I fell and broke my leg that she would call my dad at work and I would have to go to the emergency room. Those threats meant nothing, so I kept jumping anyway. I was having a blast. Until I fell. I splatted on the ground, but both my arms stretched out in front of me to break my fall. I fell hard. Suddenly, my arm worked. Just like that. No more twitching. It just worked. It was like a miracle. My mom looks at me and says, "Well, if I would have known that's all it took, I would have shoved you down a long time ago."

And just like that, my arm worked. The doctors couldn't ever figure out what caused the nerves not to function. I think it was because I needed to learn that when I fall, better things wait for me when I get back up.

Elegy Untold

MADELINE KIM, Grade 12, Age 17. Polytechnic School, Pasadena, CA.
Grace Hamilton, *Educator*

what I hate / about stars is they're not those candles / that
make a joke of cake, that you blow on / and they die and come
back, and you / you're not those candles either
—Bob Hicok, "Elegy Owed"

In the year I first discovered burnt casseroles and untied rib-
bon, my mother was convinced that jicama would save our
lives. As my siblings and I were forced to eat the most recently
proven miracle vegetable of the decade, we held our noses and
chewed slowly, letting the white slices grate against our throats
like sandpaper. We pretended that we were eating watermelon,
that we were biting into something sweet and unguilty. This is
how we survived the days summer dangled what we couldn't
have in front of us with its ungloved fingers and heavy hospital
blanket.

* * *

I first read "Elegy Owed" sitting in the grass at writing camp,
in a circle of my peers like stones around an invisible fire. A
lung / or finger, is it time / already for inventory, a mountain,

I have three / of those, a bag of hair, box of ashes. I read and reread Hicok's elegy, felt the words curdle against my tongue. I read elegies for brothers, daughters, miscarried foals, amputated limbs. I wrote elegies for people who were still alive, and I often thought of my mother. I worried that my unbridled fascination for reading about the dead meant something bigger than a love for words and regrets.

* * *

My mother would discard the lasagnas and casseroles and creamed corn distant acquaintances left on our doorstep the same way she hung roses upside-down after her mother's death: to clear the temptation of self-destruction from the air. Upon my father's breast cancer diagnosis, she desperately attempted to undo what had already been done by forcing home-squeezed carrot juice into my brother, sister, and me. She woke up, frantic, while the sky was still dark, to wash fresh carrots and celery and broccoli, to stuff them into the juicer, and to squeeze for hours. She cooked to the movement of harvest, the slow ebb and flow of separating grains. She took her own shopping cart to the farmers' market every Saturday morning and would return with overflowing bags of vegetables, and we moaned to ourselves because we knew she would make us eat them all. My father would try to fight her attempts with curses, feigned sleep, the I'm going through painful chemotherapy and surgeons will soon be slicing me open to get a glimpse at the tumor inside my left breast excuse that was countered with you can't fight through your doctor. Kenchana, mogo. It's just jicama.

At thirteen years old, with a father at stage III during the peak of America's I heart boobies fetish, this is the extent to which I understood: If I lay sprawled across a hardwood floor, the pressure might flatten my breasts. If I sat by the window, I could retrieve the Whole Foods lasagna people left on our doorstep before my mother and coddle a bite of sweet tomato sauce, savor the empty carbohydrates of the pasta sheets.

My mother, through an ironic desire to protect her children, was scathingly honest from the beginning. We should eat the kale salads and four slices of required jicama out of our own desire to live, as our chances of being diagnosed with breast cancer may be up to five times as high. As a result, I hungered for elegies, maybe to convince myself that I could salvage images of a meaningful life from my father's.

* * *

My mother is the type of woman who sobs only after everyone else has fallen asleep. Surrounded by silence, having grown up with two deaf-mute parents in the poorest area of Seoul, she took pleasure in being vocal. Perhaps after emigrating to Los Angeles and living with an uncle who resented the burden of taking her in, not knowing any English, marrying an ill-tempered college classmate, settling down to care for her parents, and watching her mother die of a brain tumor not long after her own third and last child was born, she felt like her life was finally slipping like a frayed rug underneath her. By forcing us to eat slices of jicama and sauteed spinach until one of us threw up, she held on to what she could.

* * *

The day my father came home with a stitch across his left breast, the day of his mastectomy, he declared that we should no longer believe in God. That believing in something bigger than the cards we've been dealt was pointless hope. He cradled his masculinity in the crook of his arm. He became angry and volatile because the disease that should have killed him was plastered with women in pink jogging suits, because the advertisements and charity runs and pink socks of the most widely publicized cancer excluded him completely. He would hold screaming fits with himself, driving away in the middle of the night because there was dog piss in the carpet or because my mother hadn't washed the shirt that he wanted to wear.

We would shiver in moments of silence because they were rare and unstained. My mother assumed her stance as provider, as the midwinter ice between the lake and the horizon. She read us Bible verses whenever my father drove, placeless, when he was angry. We sat on the rug in the living room and watched the cyclic motion of her lips. I remember her praying silently in her bedroom and my father punching a hole through the door and finding a chunk of wood in the bathroom trash can and the hole covered with white flypaper the next morning.

* * *

Toward the end of my father's chemotherapy, my mother returned one afternoon from the farmer's market with only a box of mangoes and a quietness in her fingertips because the man who sold her vegetables tried to kiss her. In the mornings, the house was still, and we no longer had to hold our noses as carrot juice washed down our throats. She resigned more and more often to her room, the lights off and the bedsheet corners undone.

* * *

She forgot about my birthday the day I turned thirteen. As she had been asleep for most of the morning, I didn't want to disturb her or the unusual stillness of the house she had seemed to crave. When she began to stir into motion in the afternoon, her hair disheveled and upright like the strings of released balloons, I quietly reminded her and immediately regretted it, knowing she was remorseful by the way she looked down at her hands.

* * *

Sometimes people harbor pressure the way helium fights against the skin of a balloon. My father survived with his tumor removed and a moderate case of lymphedema. He started his own law practice after losing his job and his health insurance. He left for work before we woke up and returned right before we went to sleep. He regained his composure, poised and ready to take the reins as the provider of the family.

My mother, in contrast, seemed to invert—she complained of sleep apnea and foot pain, she gained thirty pounds. Some mornings we had to pull over to the side of the road so she could rest her legs from driving. In the afternoons, she slept, and we ordered pizza or boiled instant ramen. She shrieked when we asked her questions. She burst into tears when my brother complained of not understanding his algebra homework. We hovered like satellites around her bed, and her eyes were flat and she stared out the window at the moon.

* * *

At first we were happy because we could finally eat what we wanted. But when she seemed to become numb to the weight of her hips or when she went days without speaking to us, I thought I was watching her die. She rarely finished her sentences. She ached unspecifically, throughout her entire body. My father began to react violently once more: You don't feel, you don't care, you aren't being their mother. He threw chairs at my brother when he cried because he was the only one who ever cried anymore. He bought bottled carrot juice from the grocery store because he finally began to understand what was good for him.

* * *

My mother is still distant and glazed. She is a reverberation of a sinking stone in a lake. I often think about the way she mispronounces prejudice. The stitch she bares across her stomach, reminding us of her three C-sections while my father stands close. I used to imagine myself reading her elegy at a funeral, my father in black leather shoes and crying. Now, he takes her walking at night, brings home coffee and cookies, offers to teach me how to drive—and I know he is sorry. I often read "Elegy Owed" to myself, scribbling lines into my notebooks in class whenever I get the urge to cry. I still love my mother. I still love poems for the dead, poems with fingers unblistered and palms untouched.

Womanhood

ALEAH ADAMS, Grade 12, Age 17. School of the Arts, Rochester, NY.
Ashley Perez, *Educator*

The string in between
Hangs limp from my open legs.
All of the world tugs.

Sixth Grade

WINONA SCHEFF, Grade 12, Age 17. Rockville High School,
Rockville, CT. Victoria Nordlund, *Educator*

Natural was just a lost fragrance.
Makeup refused to cover my purity.
I wore long-sleeved shirts every day, they called me Gorilla.

Romance Disguised as Portent of Doom

ALINE DOLINH, Grade 12, Age 17. Oakton High School, Vienna, VA.
Susan Sullivan, *Educator*

I fall in love the same way
deer break open on asphalt
after meet-cutes with minivans.
It's so easy to confuse
the situations—there are always
the obligatory vultures, their bodies
tar-slick and ravening. A certain charm
to the constancy of the screaming.

I stumble across the first body
while walking home. After that,
a pageant of carcasses. First
the flesh strewn unkempt
across the lawn, crimson blooms
like wayward roses. Then the flies
in Biblical swarms. It's a melody
I already know by heart.

What I'll never get used to
is the fawns themselves—
the uncanny symmetry
of infant limbs unfolding
across the driveway
in clumsy tableaux, the eyes
daydream glossy while
readying for immolation.

to do—

ALISHA YI, Grade 10, Age 15. Ed W. Clark High School, Las Vegas, NV.
Melissa Villanueva, *Educator*

I page
catcalls
on
old telephone
wires,
but
my tongue
is
dead
swollen.

On flyleafs,
we
write
autopsy
questions
in
the same
handwriting
with
blue fountain-pen
ink.

En gli sh

ALISHIA MCCOY, Grade 12, Age 17. Cleveland School of the Arts High School, Cleveland, OH. Daniel Gray-Kontar, *Educator*

so lately ive been teaching myself english and id like to point
out that i am
a writer
im is a poet okay? people come to me they say
Drama students say "Can you write my play for me pleeeease
Alishia I'll pay you?"
then i realize . . .
i didnt even know where to put the question mark typing out
that statement but anyway
I realized
I say "girl I need tah be writing a play for myself" I say "I
dont even write enough for me
I cant write enough fah da bof of us"
besides I dont know english and what if yo girl, you know/
yo character speak english i cant be hah honey I cant
I can be me and all these voices in my head but not "hah" as
Sidney would say
but anyway (again)
Im sitting here teaching myself subject verb agreement
I say
well how the hell imma know if dey agreein I dont know da
subject from da verb
and wat they'd like to agree upon dey be tryna trick you too
they give you two subjects and say make da verb agree I say I
disagree wit the subject all tah getha
why I care whether they agreein

wif each other
I mind my own business

girl imma hafta get me ah scholarship elsewhere
in another area cuz disdis
sumin
you gotta learn dis when you little i dont speaks like this
you gotta
mah mama, mah deddy they do not speak like this I cant go
in all ziggity . . . dey say ziggity boo
but imma say new all ziggity new
like i been speaking dis my whole like no!
I cannot and I will not Okay?
Hah! I just—
How are we us
you and I
you I and our people supposed to do anything
they know we dont know these things and they cant be all its
all our fault cuz it aint
mah mama she taught me what she know and she know a
whole lot but i be listenin and that's where I know how ta talk
I just listen thats all

and mah mama been listenin to her mama thats been listenin
to hers
thats been listenin to hers so you know?
thats why Im here this aint no new thang dis is us

in all our just in our all

dey shouldnt do dat to me
dey shouldnt make us hafta to make us talk like them aye

who say dey da ones that talk right anyway
we all understand each other

Whether they like it or not
 I like my english broken

Hot Comb

AMY DUNCAN, Grade 11, Age 16. Douglas Anderson School of the Arts, Jacksonville, FL. Tiffany Melanson, *Educator*

Mother yanks my
dark wet curls and
leads my head toward
the white stove. I
stand stiff, black bronze
grazes my scalp.
Clouds of gray smoke
surround us. I cough
and Mother needs
more grease.

We walk
back to master
bedroom, third trip
now, sweat piles
on my forehead, runs
down my too-wide nose.

Mother slaves
over stove,
wipes thin dark brow, slathers grease
once more, travel

back then forth,
to bedroom.
Bends my neck
toward her,

feel it crack, tug it
back, feel my back

bow when she
combs out my roots,
pulls hair in fist,
my neck bent
sideways, helps me
stumble
into kitchen.

Feel big ears burn
red and white,

cry out,

feel hot
grease
and dry
dead hair

stuck to wet neck,
comb boils oil on
dark
skin,

cold water later,
almost done now.

This is beauty:
Brush out burnt curls,
and back to white
stove and black comb

The Nosebleed Year

AVA GOGA, Grade 12, Age 17. McQueen High School, Reno, NV.
Talin Tahajian, *Educator*

No angels, no handlebars. Just elbows,
     skidmarks, scars. We lived that summer
with our fingers in our small mouths,
     like turned strawberries, unfired clay
our bodies tadpole soft. I remember,
     we didn't know how to use our hands,
sock drawers hiding our brothers'
     stolen pocket knives. Each morning
swung open like a switchblade. Inside,
     we found the wet and wriggling—
Minnows. Silverfish. Garden snakes
     caught and kept in the bathtub. I remember.
How we slipped through time like that.
     How we bled only in our sleep. I woke
to the shame of a blotched pillow, the baby fat
     of my cheeks stained the color
of a rusted-out car. That summer
     we wore spit beneath our band-aids,
threw soda cans into the street
     to watch them explode, then sucked
the spraying sugar, the sharp edges,
     anything to prove we were still
made of sweetness and heat. I remember
     how each day shut like a tongue
pressing against the roof of a mouth,
     how we found a newborn fawn,

motherless, naked, torn over asphalt
     like the smear of a comet.
In elegy, my brother dipped the body
     in gasoline and laid it down in the driveway
where neighborhood kids gathered.
     We knew, somehow, every day of our lives
had led to this—the smoke drawn and purged
     from that curled form, that curled form glowing,
the martyr of our softness.

Illegal

AVIK SARKAR, Grade 9, Age 14. Buckingham Browne & Nichols School, Cambridge, MA. Wes Williams, *Educator*

the words I'm told to say are
creases of my mouth
like
       one, two, three

their eyes see straight through
my newly starched skirt,
my skin (darker than theirs).
staring, like
don't be afraid,
       (we don't bite)

they say, oh, what
      is
your name?

(silence freezes the room)

at last, the syllables slip
from my lips like mangled
metal, and I say
     two,
        three,
           one

they sigh (and I know
     just what
I have lost)

Idyll

CARISSA CHEN, Grade 11, Age 16. Phillips Exeter Academy,
Exeter, NH. Mercedes Carbonell, *Educator*

She taught me to arrange the fake bones
      in a perfect circle, five-year-old fingers
cradling calcium as if only circles would trap the
      moon by white.
This was the summer all the girls in
      my class claimed they saw the same ghost,
the summer of burning tea leaves
      burying bibles,
the summer we listened to bleating radios
      sing of panacea. Penumbra summer and her
brother held a 9mm Ruger to the chest,
      pointed and pulled as sliding
a quarter into the Ruby Diner's gumball machine.
      Perfect blue, man-made sky, the jukebox
in the parlor singing staticky Sex Pistols
      and the salt on the fries so sweet, so sticky.
By September, the black girl's seat was
      beneath Ms. Koken's class confederate
flag and she called it *nostalgia*.

a wolf in birmingham

DANIEL BLOKH, Grade 9, Age 14. Alabama School of Fine Arts, Birmingham, AL. Iris Rinke-Hammer, *Educator*

i have woven her from sticks and straw;
pebbles for eyes, firefly
for a voice.
she has learned the night,
dissolves through it like salt—
learns human, wears it over her hunger,
learns to hide her tongue
as she walks down the street.
i let her free.
i birth my own destruction.
years later, we spot each other across the street
and smile. she takes me
to her hotel room. i sing a lullaby
as she opens her mouth
and pulls me in
through
her teeth

Fifth Generation

KEELY HENDRICKS, Grade 12, Age 18. The Harpeth Hall School, Nashville, TN. Denise Croker, *Educator*

When I was ten, I stole my first cigarette out of Father's
saddlebag
And lit it up on the hay bales with the other farmers' sons
We were all hiding
Some of us from banging a dusty pail against our red, chapped
knees
And calling in Costica, the black pig who had small eyes and
chalky toes, to supper
Others hiding from helping their raw-handed mothers clean
the vegetables
With stern faces bundled in white scarves
The cigarettes tasted sour and stunk up the barn,
But we smoked them, and threw hay at the ones who choked
When I was sixteen, I took on manhood with stupid alacrity
And joined the older boys in the sugar beet fields
I hoped the ropes would strengthen my hands like Father's
The little ones watched me jealously, and went back
To bitterly bang their bony knees with feeding pails and call
in the pigs
The first time I lit up in front of the other farmers, leaning on
the plow,
I felt like I had earned something eternal
The younger kids watched me with pout-lipped envy , then
slunk back to the barn
What I didn't realize, was that I had indeed earned something
eternal

I didn't see how the plow aged my hands,
Made my fingers like the sole of a boot, and my face like the
other men's faces
Forty years of carving these fields left furrows in our brows
as deep as the ones in the ground.
I guess I never noticed that,
There will always be more sugar beets, kids with sharp-boned
stomachs
Who scrape their knees with pails and smoke in the barn
There has been no drought of ugly black pigs with chalky feet
And red-faced mothers bundled in naframas who yell and
scrub vegetables in plastic basins
No end to the desperate fathers who make their sons men
And sons who believe them
I grin and pull out my cigarette—there has been no end to
these either
I suck in the fumes like it is my breath,
Because I've learned that their air is sweeter
When we sit on our plows and take fervent drags,
No one throws hay at each other, because we're men, and we
don't cough anymore
That's one thing that's changed

Suffering in the Form of Empty Arms

JAMISON RANKIN, Grade 11, Age 16. South Carolina Governor's School for the Arts and Humanities, Greenville, SC. Mamie Morgan, *Educator*

The drill of energy has slipped down
the kitchen drain, flowing somewhere
in the veins of iron ductile; outside,
the shumard has shed the rust of

decaying leaves. I sit at the kitchen
table, letting smothered hashbrowns
go untouched, I hear the tub fill with
water. Mother's gentle glide into

water. Mother's gentle glide into
what is lukewarm, the door locked,
remembering what was spilled the
night before: the entrails of her unborn

son on the silk of cerulean sheets.
Dad is nowhere to be found. Maybe
he's seventy-three hours away, trying
to find God on a desolate highway,

he knows the only kind of
righteousness to be received is
injecting stem cells in the arms
of the sanctified. Yet he knows

Mother is not to receive this,
she is too weak to turn her face
to the dwindling hands of the clock.
She thinks of a scrub pasture

somewhere out in Brighton, where a
farmer plays the role of an almighty,
a mother cow bellowing for her calf
that's already packaged and sitting

on ice shelves. Strength has become
depletion. There is depletion in the
glow of her skin, the way she asked
me to change the sheets on the bed.

I had to hear it for myself: the slowing
pace of her heart pulsing through the
bathroom door, the stained bedding
tumbling in the washer, Bob Seger

whispering of turning an elusive
page somewhere in a taxi cab
outside of Vancouver, Dad trying
to breathe in the lyrics, grief louder
than the monotony of absence.

Things I Always Do

MASON SMITH, Grade 9, Age 14. Colorado Academy, Denver, CO.
Betsey Coleman, *Educator*

Turn the fan on when I'm in the bathroom
Make my pencil lead too long and push it back in
Abandon books
Chew gum with my mouth open
Write in all capital letters
Sleep with too many pillows
Get too much ice in my drink
Complain about having too much ice in my drink
Type with only my pointer fingers
Forget to untangle my headphones
Sit in the backseat of the car, behind the driver
Sleep in the clothes that I wore the day before
Avoid eating cheese
Stay on sidewalks to keep the snow untouched
Eat too slowly
Have a minor cough
Stop at every stop sign on my bike
Choose the window seat on a plane
Have a messy room
Bounce my leg
Order a steak burrito at Chipotle
Think too hard
Forget to water my plants
Read the review, travel, and magazine sections of
The New York Times on Sunday
Order chocolate ice cream on a sugar cone

Dress too warm

Have too many tabs open on my phone

Walk slowly even though my legs are long

Get really interested in things that will never help me in life

Think about becoming a vegetarian

Skip the first page of a notebook

Forget how to do vibrato with my pinky finger on the cello

Take good photos on disposable cameras but not develop them

Play a song on repeat until I tune it out

Misspell lieutenant

Stare at the maps at the back of classrooms when I should be paying attention

Feel too intimidated to make direct eye contact

Lean back in my chair

Talk about the weather

Feign my interest in sports

Buy things that I'm too afraid to wear

Get overly excited for holidays

Write too much

Linguistics
(for my mother)

MAYA EASHWARAN, Grade 11, Age 16. Milton High School.
Alpharetta, GA. Marea Haslett, *Educator*

Ma, I haven't spoken Tamil in three years.
(call it forgetting, or just prenatal Americanization)
Some god must have known I was a child
of loose change, of ambiguity, of everything more confused
than it should be. Of conjoined twins snipped off
the cord together. Of the love of a language. Of everything
unbounded and shivering; Mother, maybe I'll
lose the syllables of my name next, ancient and observing,
still,
like the way rice farmers wade into their crop after the
monsoon
swallowed them whole. This is a lesson on everything sacred.
Ma, I forgot my name before I learnt how to blink. We
promised to keep culture like dollars and gum wrappers,
stashed in inside-out pockets, tumbled and dried in the wash,
bleached and chlorinated by city swimming pools, floating
pieces of ourselves blanched in cauliflower and
contamination;
this is how letters forget themselves, this is how a
daughter loses the weight of her tongue in her mouth, replaces
it with a borrowed accent, a softer l, a rumbling a, a smeared
r, toothpick consonants, dissonance. Ma, we were Indian until
we weren't. Meanwhile, I pretend I am cultured, I read
Dickinson,

structure culture around the line breaks of my own igno-
rance. Outside,
the sun melts into itself and I am thinking of all the ways to
say that I
am lost, the crumpled syllables cramping in my mouth, this
is not
poetry anymore, this is what happens when a daughter for-
gets where
her lungs are, what they were made of. Ma, I'm losing parts of
myself every day, leaving bits of human when I walk, buttons,
sweater
strings, rosin dust, crushed bottles of water, words and words
and
worlds, latex gloves and frozen-over car lots downtown,
mustard seed heat thawing immigrant dreams, silence.
I want to question whether these are the things that make up
the constellations of my genetics, the silence of my voice, but
even I
I know nothing is silent about life. I've lost more than I have
ever lost in
sixteen years. I've started shedding ethnicity like hair:
Mother,
I fear I'll go bald.

a pathologist's report at the wharf

NOEL PENG, Grade 11, Age 16. Castilleja School, Palo Alto, CA.
Anne Wagenhals, *Educator*

we begin bare-knuckled, bare-
breasted. soothe our stings with salt.

that is how we learn to hunger
for the liver. for the fish eyes anchored, souvenir
magnets cool against our cheek. what we love we grab

only with throat, swallow it whole
until stomachs oscillating and full, our lips

desperate for the skin-like. we sit, cattle boating—
our nets yanked from below the soundstage,
from electric fencing

around the perimeter. soon, we will electrocute
the bay with our catch, split down the scales for the high-end
and their bellies.

but for now, we are raw-throated; we are mouths
like bow-legged infants. wailing.
ravenous.
defected in the bone. we carry our teeth

like a history—always snatching; leave biting

to the dogs. in our youth we learned how to body a beautiful
thing:
to whittle the abdomen empty, to teach how to prey, to break
jaws
on the elbows of children for their polyester.
what we learned was all
cutthroat,

kept on suckling until stomached, the shells we spat
only for tradition. still—we hollow wharf for a fish bone
hoping the smallest chokes us.

hoping we bruise
easily, how quickly we find the knives
in our softest parts.

Series of Stutters

PARISA THEPMANKORN, Grade 12, Age 17. Morris Hills High School, Rockaway, NJ. Sara Bauer, *Educator*

where each pause is another second
spent outside your skin. Outside, the air draws a blank

whenever you inhale. You begin to take your oxygen
with a side of choking, like a twisted iron throbbing

in your stomach. I follow you into your throat, watch
as you carve train tracks on your tongue to forget,

finger swimming in tension thicker than the moments
before a car crash. How your father would finger the buckle

of his belt after Sunday mass and you knew. How on
Mondays you would wilt somewhere between Broadway

and Seventh, mouth like a siren without the sound,
pinched red from the way your father would reach

past your teeth and explore organs with a fist
heavier than the weight of your world. Once you opened a
  Bible

and watched hollow words drip from your tongue.
Dead weight. I figure there's no way around it—

New York and its concave avenues swerve like
strangleholds. I fill your bruised hands with inches of red
  wine,

a potion for you to halve your tongue and let blood leak.

All the meatless wolves in New York would howl

for an encore if you could give them one. I touch your face,
the curve of your cupid's bow. There is no hesitation

in the way you open your lips in the darkness, swell past the
        space
between the platform and the L-train, the ready ache of your
        saliva

DANTE RADYSH BOWMAN, *Building and Bodies*,
Grade 12, Age 18. The Hartsbrook School, Hadley, MA.
Cherrie Latuner, *Educator*

The Frame

SOPHIE HOOD, Grade 8, Age 13. St. Catherine's School, Richmond, VA. Tonya Walker, *Educator*

I rest on a wall
Composed by four corners of metal
Holding a precious memory inside
Every day a young girl looks at me
She watches
She cries
It's a sad joy
To have someone look at you for so long
Inside of me there is a photo of her past
A photo of days gone by
She watches because it's all she has left
She cries because she needs more
Time passes as the cracks in her skin grow wide
I see her pour herself into me
She isn't the same girl as before
Her eyes are like holes where life should have been
Her stormy blues are now dull azures
They are empty and cold
Those eyes watched life pass them by
Those eyes only wanted me

Hollow

JESSICA ZHANG, Grade 12, Age 17. Westford Academy,
Westford, MA. Rebecca Ingerslev, *Educator*

I once walked in on my blind grandfather in the bathroom.
I thought that I was missing something, that God had lent a
careless hand when he built me.

Down there was like a gutted fish, or a smallness in reverse.
Nursery school playmates would say it had fallen off in tran-
sit, and I would curse that artless stork.

I grew like the rest did—around a hollow space. Boys fished
for redemption in that void. But you would lust instead
for fullness like yours. I could offer only a hook

or silvered folds. Who was I to change you when the world
took so long allowing full to love full—when for so long you
kept this secret, who was I to break its vigil?

The need to know, the need to meet. Also empty: a cathedral,
or something like it. An ocean named human is so thin
it takes no space. We both only wanted to be filled.

I once caught a fish, about as long as you were long. Two
silver eyes stuck to me like the rain. His mouth gaped hollow,
lips open
like a prayer. Why I threw him back:

His was an emptiness
that I could understand.

Machiavelli

MARGOT ARMBRUSTER, Grade 10, Age 15. Brookfield Academy, Brookfield, WI. Karen Schleicher, *Educator*

& the lemon wept tears of
blood—i
am the rush in your mouth
the tide
of rust encroaching on your
horizons

& i said nothing—i didn't
need to
say anything—he had gone
silent
and curled up in bed with his
knife

& so i took my leave—god
be with
you—from this strange
catharsis—
the end, any end, justifies the
means.

Autobiography

STELLA BINION, Grade 11, Age 16. Payton College Preparatory High School, Chicago, IL. Leslie Russell, *Educator*

I am 11, I am beginning to feel the cotton in my mouth
it teaches me to think before I speak
My mouth starts to learn what feels good
I've always liked the way the words "black body" fall from my
lips
I like to say them aloud
I keep those words quiet, because I don't know if they apply
to me
I only know the papery pigment of a family I do not see myself
reflected in,
but my black is as undeniable as my mother's white

I am 11 and have learned that there are mysteries burned into
my skin
I do not have the privilege of clear white blood coursing with
names, hometowns, birth dates, families kept together
My aunties only speak in three generations
they tell me
we come from grandma Martha and grandfather Earl
growing in gardens and church hall pews
deep in Mississippi
where white spit touched their dark skin
like the wake of water hitting boats carrying dark skin
I want to know what shores I come from
so I don't have to explain
why I only know where my mother's great-great-grandfather

grew up
why only half of me is precious
why the missing marks of my lineage lay so deep on my skin
that
I'm too dark to believe only German

I am learning that ancestry.com doesn't track the bloodlines
left by whips
I am European conquest
or maybe just my father is

I am 11 when I always become the person to look at
when it's the color black
And I don't know what to do besides smile back
because I don't know what inside of me
or who before me
gives me the right to do anything else

When I am 16,
no longer knees to heaving chest, connecting my black body to
my heartbeat
bringing myself deeper into the tissues that created me
I will instead sleep with my feet out
so I dream of walking on soil and not on cement
so there are no cracks in my foundation
so I travel from what I am, to what I still must be
with every cottonseed, raindrop, blood drop, tear
of every ancestor beneath me

I will ask my 16-year-old self what my history is
She must answer
I am creating it

The Author Spots Charlie Parker Outside of an Unspecified Subway Stop in NY, NY

DAVID EHMCKE, Grade 12, Age 17. East High School, Sioux City, IA.
Wendy Bryce, *Educator*

and as I spotted him I was a whirlwind of star-struck fear
and he was an ocean of unburied caskets and he was weary
of everything unfamiliar and I could see the real bird and
his fear stuck to his bones and shivered like a salt fish trying
to understand air and it can be scary to spot a man halfway
through his own beheading similar to seeing the wounds you
inflicted on a loved one unknowingly I can tell he wishes to
flee but he has the work of an entire generation bolting him
to this moment and the actions that I took were out of pure
sorrow and there was no label to give the act a label is merely
a borrowed existence and I wished to give him something
I took his flask and busted it into a jagged bear claw I cut a
small burrow into my stomach and invited him to make a
home of it I stared Charlie warmly in his eyes and spat—jump
inside this world is a mystery but it is yours to explore turn
this raw clay into a palatable piece of art bird find refuge here
with me and the world will be ours don't you know I'd do
anything to stay here with you

The Fifth Series of Red

ASHLEY GONG, Grade 12, Age 17. Newtown High School, Sandy Hook, CT. Michelle Toby, *Educator*

In deep-throated Julys, boys pray for
legs that don't tremble in Midwestern fields

where a father shoots a deer and skins it
in front of his son whose hands shake

with the primal rush of murder,
from witnessing the most ancient of tests

played out in the rural classroom of Arkansas
where boys learn how to clench their fists

in fetal position, how to clean the blackened
lungs of an M-76, and how to shoot a deer

so that it collapses into itself,
nature's morbid form of origami.

It's a boyhood of rituals, of learning how to build
a throne in the jungle gym, of his father handing

him the gun, which, despite all its stoic power,
felt dead in his hands, a limp carcass slack in his arms,

the steel arteries drained of all impulse for life.

Just him and a dead man, out in the woods
for his 16th birthday, his father swollen and red-faced

shouting instructions into the womb of the sky
which hung cocooned in tapestries of clouds.

Him and the gun pressed into the knot of his chest,
fingers flighty and nerves delicate like lace. Nothing

but the backwards surge into his chest, the bloody dawn
dripping, a period of unborn words. Him missing

his target by a good foot, the deer lurking
in thick tufts of oaks strung like woodland hair.

His father swearing, fleshy mouth twitching
with all that lies unsaid, just another fallen king

from the assembly line of mass-produced men:
firm jaws, eyes that bite at chokeholds,

boys who drink to become clean, who cup
the moon's reflection in their hands and down it

like silvery absinthe. Not him whose hands still stutter
when the gun stammers back, chatters into his body,

who spends an entire evening afterward washing
his hands in bloated sinks until they turn up raw,

naked with christening. It isn't until 9 pm
that he comes in my Chevy and we drive along

the collarbone of the Atlantic, watching as the moon
melts away to a crescent in a sky smeared with mascara,

all the stars dark as bullets. Him in the front seat,
wringing his hands as if to choke the answer

out of his palms, waiting for the moment
when it is neither night nor dawn and his father

emerges from the garage, fists red like lipstick.

The Resurrection

ANNA LANCE, Grade 12, Age, 17. West High School, Anchorage, AK.
Temperance Tinker, *Educator*

I. MARY. Stayed at home. The rooms bundled
with mourning, memories shared around
bites of barley bread, tossed and chattered
conversation. The swing of eyes leaned
against her as she moved through
with the earthenware milk and spirits.
Your brother was a good man they'd say.
Good before God and before men. She'd nod
and smile around the bright pressure
like seeds and flour burning in her throat
or watered wine on dry ground. Would try
not to duck the caresses on her hair,
recalling the sweet dark stickiness,
how little she minded cleaning out
the symbolic gunk of road-dust
once she'd knelt and washed His feet.

II. MARTHA. Met Him on the road.
Heart a skinned rabbit revitalized,
bloody and fitful, its feet hammering.
His shape a form of color and shadow
with the faithfuls at his heels. The first word
out of her mouth was Lord but the rest
of her sentence said why. His answers:
frustratingly analgesic to the heat of
desperate grief, allowing her to cool

her forehead against the railings
of His irreproachable logic. Mouth all acid.
Disciples silent. Yes, you are the Messiah
son of God the resurrection and the life
she said and let Him feel as a convulsion
in the Bethany midday burn the resolution,
as they stood there, raw and shifting
but you let him die.

III. JESUS. Felt very tired. Knew
what had to be done, and what couldn't.
Followed the sisters with a heavy step
to the tomb. Thought about homilies
and ineffable purpose and how much
it hurts to love a man tenderly and have him leave
and rend their small world with his leaving.
How undoing is not the same as preventing
the ever having done. How alive he used to come
in daylight, the ruck of the scythe-scar on
his smile and his carefully displayed doubts,
the talks they'd have about what happens
when you die and how to prove the unprovable
and how perfect he was in his willingness
to learn. Salt of the earth and spark of the sun.
Saw the sisters crying, and the stone nudged
almost casually to shield the yawning mouth
of the full-bellied cave. Covered His face
with His hands. Wept.

IV. LAZARUS. Woke up. Startled first
by the smell of four days' worth
of his own decay. Then the spiced linen

on his lips and nose and eyes and
the regretful curve of his back as if
he'd spent the night in a bad
position. Then: the sounds. Mary Martha
he wanted to say, speech fighting forward
slow as sleepwalking but not even
in the stale nothing that had removed him
unceremoniously from his love did he dare
to think the other name. Realized suddenly
that he was no longer sick. Heard
the hoarse cry, shuddering low for some reason
Lazarus come out! Followed His command.
Did not understand. Take off the grave clothes
and let go. Felt the shroud fall and his brain
fill with fire. Saw light.

a posthumous exploration of middle America

RYLEE BLACK, Grade 11, Age 16. Olympus High School, Salt Lake City, UT. Angie Van Berckelaer, *Educator*

q: do you remember that night
a: which night
q: the long one in the dakotas
a: of course
q: what was it like
a: i found gold in the hills
i stood in the Missouri
i spoke to blizzard ghosts
q: the roaming ones
a: no in the schoolhouse
q: so you've left
a: yes i live above now
like in a bubble
q: how's that
a: bright
q: like the moon
a: this isn't performance art i'm really not coming back
q: so where are you going
a: i don't make promises
q: a destination is a promise
a: a tether
q: ah well that's all
we have no more time
a: thank you

When Told Not to Chronicle Eroticism
—after Mary Szybist

AIDAN FORSTER, Grade 10, Age 15. Fine Arts Center, Greenville, SC.
Sarah Blackman, *Educator*

If I were a classical nude, the distance
between my nipples would be

the same as from my nipples
to my belly button, the same distance

from there to the split head
of the pelvis. The body: quiet bone

construct can be charted
in the faults of its architecture.

When the eggs of a Japanese carp are endangered,
the male will suck them into his mouth

and hold them. His mouth, master imitator
of womb, makes teeth from them.

He spits them out like they are dead, finds
a new mate. To begin in the middle

he spits them out like they are dead.

Once, my mother and father slicked
their bodies together, tried to see

how far inside of each other
they could get. Maybe my father put

his fingers inside my mother's mouth.
They attempted to create one body

from two. My father: root/glacier/bone.
My mother: earth/ocean/socket.

Gilgamesh taught bodies to fear themselves.
His own body: a ziggurat, a spirit trap.

From animal spirits the gods made a man,
Enkidu. Enkidu drank the milk-rivers

of the beasts, ate the greenness of the earth.
A temple prostitute offered her body to him

in supplication. He entered her, did not exit
for seven days. Afterwards, he was so split

from beasts that he could do nothing
but become a ziggurat too.

I cannot chart the moment
when I left boyhood. My bones

had not finished growing,
only stuck their pale heads

into the light of my flesh
and opened their mouths.

Death Is Linear
(Time Is Negotiable)

CAMERON KELLEY, Grade 12, Age 17. Harborside Academy,
Kenosha, WI. LuAnn Underwood, *Educator*

When she was pregnant, my mom ate a clock every morning. For those seven-and-a-half months, she craved nothing for breakfast but oatmeal with butter, and my pa would make it for her every day, stirring it with his thick metal ladle. He would wait until he couldn't hear the ticking of the hands going round and round, and then he'd serve it up to her in my grandmother's ceramic bowl.

When we were seven, our babysitter, a soft-faced girl named Lily, served me and my sister tomato soup. She used the same bowls my father had, and the same ladle my father had, but the recipe didn't ask for clocks, just tomatoes and milk. Still, I ate it all.

My sister didn't touch her lunch. Instead, as she watched me eat mine, she said, "Grew up with three siblings." This was a game my sister loved, and I loved my sister.

I flipped through the book of Lily's future, looking for something interesting to share. Lily was sixteen, and at the age of seven that felt like ages, like death had to be right around the corner, but her After stretched on and on. Most of it was full of boring people and boring classes, boring excitement, and boring grief.

"Oh," I said finally. "Her first husband stops loving her when she's old."

"Her daddy won't buy her things like he'll buy her brother things. It happens all the time."

"She hits her baby, just once." I could see the act through the fog of the future, see Lily reaching out a hand to hurt a little girl who didn't look too much unlike me. I frowned up at her. "That's not a very nice thing to do, you know."

Lily, who I don't think meant to do bad things, but instead just got stuck in them like so many people do, stared at me, and smiled wrong for the rest of the day. Our next babysitter couldn't cook, but she brought us cookies from her favorite bakery down the road, so it was OK.

* * *

When my grandmother's mother was pregnant with her, she made noodles out of the dust from the mountains. They were aubergine-colored, my grandmother always said, and they were eaten with alfredo sauce.

When I was ten, my grandmother took me into the forest at dusk. My father worried, about wolves and bobcats and twigs in the path, but my grandmother didn't listen. She said the mountains protected their own. She held my hand until we were surrounded by trees and night, and I knew it was true.

My sister didn't like the forest, and my sister definitely didn't like the mountains. My grandmother told me about the Iroquois, about the settlers who kidnapped the mountains from them, and about the stubbornness of their rock. Whenever she spoke about these soft structures and their history, it was as if she saw them as people. My sister saw them as inconvenient, and spent the entire trip playing a clapping game I had been obsessed with a few weeks before. Her clapping finally got so loud it reverberated inside my head, and I shoved at her with my elbow to get her to stop.

"You're being a nuisance," I hissed, trying to listen as my grandmother said something about the story behind Cherokee Rose's. I had just learned the word, and I was proud that I had found a time to use it.

"Well, you're being a jerk." This was also a new word, picked up from cable TV.

"Be quiet, you two." I have never known my grandmother to yell, and she didn't then. But I had never known her to glare either, and she did, right at the space where my sister's eyes were. "Addy, if you could, would you tell me about flame azalea?"

I beamed, glad to have been picked over my sister. "Flame azalea, also called wild honeysuckle, is a poisonous plant found in the Appalachian Mountains, and is thought to be one of the most common versions of azalea grown by the Native Americans."

"Good job," said my grandmother.

"Suck up," muttered my sister.

They'd never really gotten along.

* * *

When she was pregnant, my mom and my pa moved to Virginia, to be closer to my grandmother. The Allen family had lived in Virginia for longer than there'd been a Virginia, their children tied to the trees and mountains in the same way my mom tied her children to time. There's a picture of my mom and pa standing in front of the house where they raised me, a flat to the ground, robin's-egg-colored thing perfect for new parents.

The mountains rise, purple and green, in the background, and there's enough life that I know it's spring. There's a picture, too, of my grandmother in the house. She's in front of the fireplace, sitting in what I think of as my pa's armchair. The quilt in her lap is one she gave to my mother, for good luck. It's made of yarn the same color as the mountains. Her feet don't even touch the floor, but the drooping skin on her face is trying to.

I liked to trace the lines in these photos. I thought that those younger, happier versions of my parents were waving at me and not the camera. After my grandmother died and my mom burned the quilt, I thought that maybe if I touched the picture of her enough times, I would start to feel the rough yarn under my fingers, smell the vanilla of her perfume. I liked what photographs could tell me.

When I was 13, photographs betrayed me. Before my parents could stop him, my middle school principal, a balding man with thin lips, shoved last year's yearbook toward me. He had decided that I had become too old for imaginary friends.

"The administration has put up with this long enough," he told me.

I watched sweat slide down the skin above his upper lip and said nothing.

"It was fine when you were a child, but you are going to be going to high school next fall. You have to know I only want what's best for you, don't you? You won't survive in high school if you don't let go of this ridiculous fantasy."

I thought of my sister, sitting in the uncomfortable Bad Kids chairs outside the office, and said nothing.

"Don't just sit there, Addy, please. I had the greatest respect for your grandmother, and I understand that losing her must have affected you greatly, but this is not how you should cope." I thought about his daughter, who was in the grade below mine, and who was going to run away to Los Angeles in four years. She was what they would come to call "troubled." I suppose they saw me now like they were going to see her later. I said nothing.

His voice got softer. "I'm going to schedule the appointments with the counselor for your Tuesday lunches. I've heard you don't really talk to anyone at lunch, so you won't be missing much, will you?"

My middle school had always had terrible air-conditioning. True heat is impossible to understand until you've lived through the sticky, sweet-tea air of a Virginia summer. For us, September was just beginning to wake up, and moving was like wading through a marsh. I watched him wipe dampness from his face with a yellowed handkerchief and I said nothing.

He slid the yearbook closer to me, and set a granola bar down next to it. "I'll be right back. Take a look at this." I watched him stand up and said, "Please don't do this to me."

While I was no stranger to the principal's office, the principal and I had never become very close. He didn't know how much I hated it when anyone touched my hair, and so he reached out and set a clammy palm on it, ruffling it a little. Then, he left.

I waited until I couldn't wait any longer. The cover of the yearbook was soft and shiny, the pages hardly worn. The seventh-grade class was halfway through the book, and my picture was one of the first. There was Rufus Akerman, whose name had rested right above mine on the roll call since elementary school. There was me, my hair pulled back in barrettes and my gap-toothed smile. I knew what I was going to see to my left before I looked, and I knew it would not be a picture of my sister.

The door opened, and the principal came back in. I watched him frown at me as I stared at the yearbook; watched him close it and take the granola bar, uneaten, and switch it out with a bottle of water; and let him walk me to the hallway, where my sister was waiting for me.

She shot up from her chair and came up close to me. "What'd he talk about? Are you in trouble again?" I said nothing.

* * *

When she was pregnant, my mom expected twins. She and my pa picked out the names—Addy and Alexi—from a little "name your baby" book, bought us matching cribs and clothes, and told anyone who would listen about us. Even some who wouldn't listen. We were their two little wonders.

When me and my sister were born, our hearts beat like a sad song's drum line. We were flimsy paper held together with old glue, our arteries made of rusty copper. Only one of us survived the week at the hospital, and when the nurse gave my mom the news, they told her my sister died holding my hand.

My grandmother used to tell me that was why I was so much unlike myself sometimes.

* * *

When I was too young to measure my life in months, they buried my sister in a pretty wooden box. She was exactly like me, a carbon copy, except for the parts of her that didn't work. After the funeral, my parents refused to talk about her, and I have to respect how well they stuck to that, even when I held conversations with a girl named Alexi that they could not see.

When I graduated high school, I went to the graveyard and sat cross-legged at my sister's grave. Her gravestone was not new and not old. It was my age.

Barely begun and already world heavy. On the stone, the same year etched twice held the grief of young parents.

"Liked fire and fast cars and other dangerous things," said my sister, in a stronger version of her voice. She was talking about the girl buried next to her, who lived for only twenty years, who had been reckless in a way I didn't like thinking about.

"That's no fun," I said back, uncomfortable now. The game wasn't played like this. "I don't like it when they've got no After."

"You like me," my sister said.

"That's different."

"You're not going to leave me alone now, are you," she asked me. I could sort of make her out, sitting with her back to the stone that marked her grave, face turned up to catch the sun. I would have thought it would be the opposite, that she would be easier to see than ever while this close to her tiny, fragile baby body, but what did I know. My powers had never extended into death.

"Of course not."

"I think I'm going to like community college."

"Yeah. I think I will too."

* * *

When she was pregnant, my mom ate a clock every morning. For those seven-and-a-half months, she craved nothing for breakfast but oatmeal with butter, and my pa would make it for her every day, stirring it with his thick metal ladle. He would wait until he couldn't hear the ticking of the hands going round and round, and then he'd serve it up to her in my grandmother's ceramic bowl.

When I was sixteen, empty and suspended in my mourning, free-falling in my grief, I destroyed every plate and bowl my mother owned. It was cruel, and I regretted it the minute I looked down at the remains of the pottery at my feet.

My mom burst into the kitchen, drenched from the shower she'd been taking. They'd always worried about me more than they would have if I was normal, I think. There was a frantic fear in her eyes.

"Look what you've done now," said the ghost of my twin sister, sitting on the countertop. She was hurting as much as I was, but she didn't have the solid hands with which to hold the cutlery.

"Why did you let her leave me," I demanded of my mother. I meant my grandmother, I meant Alexi. I didn't know who I meant, just that I was lonely.

"I didn't—"

"Why did you never talk about it, why didn't you say something." That was cruel too. I had known. I had always known. My mom was just a person. People don't always know how to let secrets slip, not without making it clear what they are.

"Oh, baby." My mom just sounded sad. I couldn't tell why, why she wasn't angry or upset about the damage I had done, not until I tasted salt and felt hot liquid down my cheeks. She strode forward and wrapped me in her arms, dripping water all over the tile and getting my shirt wet too. "Baby, I'm so sorry."

I snuck a look at my sister, and she looked wistful.

* * *

When my mother was pregnant, she had just wanted two daughters who were masters of time. So many people want what is best for their children, and just don't know how to give it to them. My mother never wanted a day to run away from us.

Now, I cannot run away from my sister.

I have never looked at my own After. I am too worried about what it will look like. Worried that it will read like my sister's novel, and not my own.

MAKENZI CARLGREN, *Rosie and Ruth*, Grade 12, Age 18,
Salina High Central, Salina, KS. Larry Cullins, *Educator*

Sullivan and the Postman

LUC LAMPIETTI, Grade 11, Age 17, Phillips Academy, Andover, MA.
Thomas Kane, *Educator*

The English bulldog would be extinct without the advent of the caesarian section. Humanity has domesticated the English bulldog in a mere 200 years to the point that pregnant members of the species rely on the operation as a result of their purposely bred, gargantuan-sized head. A head bred to satisfy human's absurd demands, rendering the English bulldog utterly inept without humanity. That's domestication for you. In this regard, the English bulldog is most akin to the generation of Bernard Sullivan.

With a shapeless face of overlapping folds and wrinkles, he resembled an English bulldog. Each time he snarled, which he did often, his lips would lift to reveal putrid, yellowed teeth. The clothes he wore were tattered and frayed, mangy and moth-eaten. His corpulence had emerged triumphant and spilled over the lapsed walls of his waistband; demanding that he left his pants unbuttoned and his fly down. He had feebly combed, but ultimately scraggly, hair and burnished blue eyes.

Presently, they were mere slits withdrawn behind puffed-up eyelids. He took another drag from his blunt. Setting it on the coffee table, he rummaged for his laptop in the rubbish at his feet. Cardboard shipping boxes, plastic wrapping, mildewed Tupperware containers with their contents spilled onto rumpled-up tees, and cigarette butts littered the apartment. The blunt continued to smolder, and the tendrils of smoke lingered in the fetid, stale air; the product of the fermented carton of milk left out on the countertop.

With a grunt and a brief belch, he propped the laptop open on the expanse of his lap. Already open to Amazon.gov, he dictated a list of items to the shopping cart: "2 gallons of 2% milk, Folgers's Instant Coffee, Minute Rice, 1 ounce of sativa . . . oh, and eggs too."

Four minutes passed. A thump issued from the front of the apartment and, in turn, a soothing, programmed British voice piped up, "Your package has arrived, enjoy!" Yet he told himself he would retrieve it in an hour or so. In the meantime, he ran his fingers over his scalp and, with what effort he could muster, tried to part the crusted strands of hair that had become integrated with the patchy locks of his beard—a composition of canned tomato sauce and drool that engendered a wretched, inescapable odor. By now he had grown accustomed to it.

In his infinite boredom, he resorted to surveying the filth of his apartment. Were one to walk about, he would assuredly be mistaken as part of the couch, an ingrained part of the rumpled laundry and packaging remnants. The paint was peeling in the recesses of the ceiling. He watched with a bemused expression as a flake languidly drifted down and landed on the rotting stalks of his potted sunflower plants.

"Ha! No maintenance my ass!" He chuckled, recalling the packaging on the box that still stood discarded to the side of the withered stalks. It read in vibrant, block letters, SELF-WATERING! NO MAINTENANCE! JUST WATCH THEM

BLOOM! It was his fault it died, though. He admitted that. The overhead light fixtures were supposed to supply natural light that supplanted the ambience of being outdoors. What is more, they were purportedly capable of growing plants too. Although he had been curious if such was veritably true, he thought them to be too damn bright and had hurled his shoe at the fixtures within a week of their installation.

Now, the only light source was the fluorescent emissions of the TV, which spanned the width and height of the wall before him. The whole setup likened itself to Winston Smith's apartment in Orwell's *1984*, but there was no intrusive Big Brother monitoring the activity, or lack thereof, in Bernard's apartment. Frankly, the government just didn't care.

With the advent of Amazon.Prime.Now.Instantly, nobody had any reason to venture out of his or her apartment, so nobody did. Prepackaged meals, diapers, elastic clothing . . . all the necessities and amenities needed of a humdrum, banal but comfortable existence could be at one's door within minutes. The diapers soon became a requisite for infants and adults alike on account of the spike in obesity. Marketing consultants noted an unprecedented shift in consumer purchases; the cosmetics and clothing lines went belly-up, as did car dealers and gas-pumps. The public went for sweats instead of suits. Perhaps this phenomenon could have been attributed to the absence of social pressure since nobody interacted, but the consultants were laid off and traded in for machines before they could publish the data.

And in the lull that followed, in which the unemployed had not yet shifted from the couches to the streets, from lamenting a lack of income to looting the local shops, construction crews of blue-jumpsuited figures began to file through the city streets. Buildings were gutted of windows and doors. Rickety screen doors and handsome oak doors alike were launched from balconies into truck beds below. Window frames were filled with semi-opaque Plexiglas, and the government men afforded each flat a Wi-Fi router and the same type of light fixtures that Bernard so detested. Just before rounding the corner, the blue-jumpsuited figures installed the same door in every doorway of the block.

The men proceeded to affix by sizeable steel bolts the iconic Amazon smile just above what seemed to be a built-in doggy door intended for packages.

As with most aspects of life, Bernard elected to ignore it. Between the renovated windows and the updated Wi-Fi, he made no fuss that the locks were now affixed to the street-facing side of the doors.

The ensuing weeks witnessed plummeting crime rates and a respite in common cold and flu cases, but soon enough, the news agencies too went belly-up. The insipid state of lethargy did not make quality news coverage. Sometimes, when Rent Day came around, the amusing news tidbit of somebody who had been devoured by their cats circulated through the city by means of Messages and Twitter. Otherwise, the public entertained themselves with reruns of past soaps.

* * *

Outside, a cackling madman hobbled up and down the sidewalk. A crippled geriatric whose pygmy lineage had kept him close to the ground. This cackling sack of bones, albeit quite lean in comparison to the modern American man, shuffled up the steps to Bernard Sullivan's apartment. A loosely fitted postman outfit dared to swallow him up and his one-strap mailbag dragged along the pavement by his feet.

A resounding series of thumps reverberated through the dense air of the apartment.

"Yur packidge has 'rived, injoy!" he hollered in a mockery of the automated British machines.

"Huh?" Bernard paused from picking the enclaves of his naval to cock an ear toward the doorway. Nothing else came, and so, with an effort that mimicked an iceberg cleaving from a glacier, he succeeded in pushing himself off of the couch. He unsurely and ungainly made his way to the door, having momentarily forgotten how to walk. Not able to peer past opaque windows, he began to retreat toward his couch when he heard a soft click. He hadn't seen the door open in roughly two decades.

Reversing direction, he shuffled back to the now ajar door.

No sooner had he inched his head out from behind the doorframe than he was yanked off his feet and hurled onto the pavement. With that, the postman hastily threw his weight against the steel door until the lock mechanism retorted with a muffled click. The entire strength and agility of the postman's movements seemed near impossible with his diminutive size. Then, without a word, he nimbly leaped over the gargantuan mound of blubber that was Bernard Sullivan and proceeded to pull the same shenanigans on the next stoop.

Meanwhile, Bernard collected himself and shifted his rump onto the steps of the stoop. Semi-faint and already perspiring heavily, he glanced up and down the street. All along the pavement sat hunched figures. Some of them listlessly twirled their thumbs, but the majority squatted with a dejected manner and their heads dropped in their laps. The streets were bleak and gray, offering no source of neon, flashing distraction. The pulsations of his heartbeat drowned his ears and inhibited him from making any sense of his situation. He was even only faintly aware in his stupor that the postman had succeeded in locking out four other occupants further up the street. And so, with that, Bernard Sullivan joined the silent ranks and let his head drop into his lap as he waited for somebody to let him back into the confines of his apartment.

A half-hour later, he heard a gunshot. Further up the street, he made out the splayed body of the postman. But his focus was quickly diverted by the front of police. With semi-automatics breaching the barrier of police shields, the unit approached the crumpled figure. Verifying his lifeless state, the front line proceeded to shed their body armor and firearms into the bed of the police vehicle. Meanwhile, the rest of the unit, which was found to be dressed in simple khakis and blue vests, continued to shuffle up the street.

At each housing unit, a few would break off from the mass and herd the residents into their respective homes. The police would then insert the key and double-check that the door was locked.

Soon the mass had made their way to the base of Bernard's stoop. Two police split from the mass and casually jogged up the steps toward Bernard. Each pressing a hand to his back, the two police ushered Bernard into the dark recesses of his apartment. Though the two police were dwarfed in relation to Bernard's size, no force was needed to escort him past the threshold of his doorway. The police knew that nothing pleased Bernard, or for that matter, any of the other block's residents, more than forsaking this dreary stoop of sullen faces to return to the musty, warm state of their apartments.

Once the last inch of Bernard had squeezed past the doorway, the police hurriedly locked the steel door. Following the click, an envelope was slipped through the doggy door and slid onto the previous package. It read, quite simply, "Apologies for the inconvenience." Inside were a couple of codes for online coupons, each stamped with the canary-yellow Amazon smile.

Romeo

JENNIFER PARK, Grade 11, Age 17. Bergen County Academies,
Hackensack, NJ. Richard Weems, *Educator*

She woke up to find the sword in her closet again. The sword
sat where her sweaters used to, shining in an empty white. It
was a plain sword, made entirely of metal with no jewels em-
bedded in the pommel or intricate guards plated in gold. The
blade was thin with a simple symmetry.

She knew better than to close the door now. Her shoulder
still ached from the first time. She took her daily shower and
halfheartedly dried her hair before using the damp towel to
grasp the hilt of the sword.

She bundled up the sword in the towel before tossing it into
the dumpster of the Harry's Diner on her way to school.

She sat down in homeroom with her hair still damp and un-
brushed.

The next morning, the sword was back in the closet. All of
her shoes were gone. She had walked into homeroom wearing
a ratty pair of her mom's too-big sneakers and her hair wet
enough to soak through the top of her T-shirt.

Voices whispered to her from the forest as she walked home.
She decided to forgo her usual shortcut through the woods and
walked the long way around through a sleepy commercial district.

She got home twenty minutes later than usual, and in the moment between when she unlocked the front door and locked it again behind her, the television screen shattered in a flurry of colored sparks.

She went up to her room and lit a candle instead of bothering to try her desk lamp. Her math homework was completed squinting by a flickering flame. As she went to bed, she played music on her battery radio in an attempt to drown out the hum of a language that she could not understand emanating from her window.

She woke up to find her window open, the casing of her radio cracked by vines, and a shelf in her closet gone. The sword floated in midair.

For once, the boy who sat next to her in homeroom did not comment on her wet hair. However, he did comment on her heavily bandaged hands. She lied rather poorly, something about hot pans and boiling water. He didn't press the issue; that was enough.

The next Monday, her hair was still wet, but the swaths of gauze that had wrapped her hands were gone, leaving behind only pink skin. The boy noticed; he did not comment.

She woke again to see that the pinkness had faded, leaving behind a strip of translucent flesh across her palms. It cemented her decision to wear gloves. They took her gloves two days after.

By the time October came, she had run out of towels and the only clothes she had left were two pairs of jeans, a single T-shirt and a rather impractical dress that she'd had to buy for that one friend's birthday party back in California.

The vines on the walls appeared when there were no longer any shelves to take. A lush moss grew out from the floor of her closet to right before the foot of her bed. That was what came afterwards. The longer she sat in front of her closet with the door wide open, the more her hair lightened and the more angular her face became.

Someone asked if she had dyed her hair the day before. Yesterday, the boy who sat next to her in homeroom hadn't recognized her for a good five seconds. When he finally did, he asked where her sudden interest in colored contact lenses came from. When she checked the bathroom mirror afterwards, her eyes had faded from an unremarkable brown to a light gray.

Whispers followed her around the school. She knew. Most weren't even particularly subtle.

Today, her attempt to dry her hair with the sheets met limited success. Her attempts to find the few clothes she had sequestered around her room met significantly less. Now she sat in front of her closet with only her duvet wrapped around her body.

Greenery and the faint sound of birdsong surrounded her. Her bedroom door and windows were blocked off by old-growth forest. The only light came in the form of the dull glow emanating from her closet.

She was being strong-armed into a contract. She couldn't think of a way to avoid it any longer. Maybe she could burn a hole through the bushes at her door; she brought the matches up a while ago. But she couldn't muster the energy to search for them.

The moss was soft and welcoming underneath her feet. She was tired.

The duvet fell from her shoulders as she grasped the hilt of the sword. The birdsong became deafening. She barely noticed when the vines rose and consumed her.

A Second Reformation: How Our World Evolved Into "Heaven on Earth"

SAMANTHA TIMMERS, Grade 12, Age 17. Scott High School,
Taylor Mill, KY. Ashley Gore, *Educator*

Comments from Professor Mariana Norvett
Fiction & Its Influence 306-005
31 January 2310:
Grade: 82 (B)
Criticism: While the essay does, for the most part, concisely
and accurately reflect Good Hope's influence on society, some
lapses in judgment and citations have been marked and sent
back to the author in an electronic copy. Surface errors include
lengthy (and thus distracting) sentence structures as well as
inadequate commentary and analysis of the issues and Hope's
influence on them. However, a clear dedication to the topic
was apparent (although note that in future papers such bias
will not be tolerable) and possibly saved the final grade from
becoming a lower score.

* * *

Jane Warbler

Professor M. Norvett

Fiction & Its Influence 306

16 January 2310

A Second Reformation: How Our World Evolved Into "Heaven on Earth"

As the dawn of the twenty-first century passed, sociologists claimed that the world had entered its second Renaissance period. Technology was abuzz with the latest cinematic techniques, providing the most realistic experience to battle foes and fly on magic carpets. "Smartphones," handheld devices that enabled people to "call" one another across vast distances (extra charges were tacked on for overseas communication, a clever ploy that was eradicated with the introduction of the cheaper, more efficient Telepath-Communicator that was invented in 2256), as well as promote the use of social media, seemed to be the cornucopia of advanced technological thinking: Never before had a piece of technology been able to fulfill a person's daily activities and chores. Unfortunately, these devices were also used to embellish one's life on various websites. Video games were constantly modified to create a more vividly "real" adventure for children and adolescents (Ketter). It seemed that the entire world was striving to become a fictional character out of a fairy tale, drunk on the thought of a glorious and magical* life.

This fad was undoubtedly dangerous and threatened the infrastructure of every major political power in the world. But there was one man who saw behind the global desire to become a fantasy. His name was Good Hope, a name that has resonated with people for decades since the beginning of his influence in 2239. An expert speaker and profound writer, Hope achieved the unachievable: worldwide enlightenment. Starting with highlighting society's achievements and then critiquing its faults, Good Hope was the start of an age where individuals could reach their full potentials, simply by eroding away their dreams. By eradicating religion and literary fiction and promoting Truth and Realism, Hope paved the way for a new age of Progressivism.

Until 2276, religion had been recognized as a major factor contributing to civilization. Often a required topic taught in schools, religion was an impossible and frustrating topic to argue about. Throughout the twenty-first, twenty-second, and part of the twenty-third centuries, when asked to explain one's actions or reasons, the most famous and common reply was "In the name of God!" When the opposing party attempted to apply reason, they were often met with backlash and criticism of being close-minded and unaccepting of others' beliefs and values (Garde). Up until more-efficient methods for book printing became feasible, the most read (or, if the person was in the lower class, the only read) book in Western civilization was the "Bible," a book that not only claimed that there was a "heavenly" being who ultimately decided every fate in the universe, but also encouraged society to worship this higher power, who was very simply named God (this is where the long-standing expression "Oh my God!" came from.) Some people made their entire livelihoods from this book, becoming "priests" or "nuns" dedicated to activities such as prayer and fasting in an elaborate display of reverence for this untestable force (Ketter).

The eastern side of the world did not fare much better, oftentimes dedicating themselves toward the worship of several gods (the longest-standing religion in this polytheistic practice was called Hinduism.) This "spiritual" practice ultimately inhibited efficient workflow practices; the obsession to maintain a "peaceful and centered" mind was proven to decrease work and study time by 16 percent, according to a survey by the Global History Bureau. By integrating themselves in this time-wasting lifestyle**, society came perilously close to Oblivion: a state in which there was no longer any divide between Fantasy and Reality. To remedy this, Good Hope rose to become a major political figure and could then spread his influence throughout the world. Before enforcing the Act of Goodwill and the Freedom Law in 2270 and 2273, respectively, Hope brought society to Reality with a series of impactful speeches. His most famous one, spoken in 2269 in Moscow, is excerpted here: "Say I take an orange, hide it behind my back, and say with the utmost conviction that it's an apple. Do you believe it's an apple? (murmured "no's" from the audience) Of course not! Then why should you believe it when someone says that there's someone out there who can cure the blind with only willpower, or can multiply a few loaves of bread into thousands with that same willpower? Science cannot lie; only people have that ability."

Hope performed this same mastery with literary and technological fiction (video games and the like). Now an international sensation, Hope was close to becoming "worshipped" himself; so in 2277, he used his popularity and spoke out against "these words that act as a disease, infiltrating the mind and then rotting it at the core." Old literary legends such as William Shakespeare, F. Scott Fitzgerald, J.K. Rowling, and Mark Twain were from then on no more (Mastoy).

In 2279, after the Truth for Cash campaign was enacted, Good's followers (which comprised the majority of the global population by then) were only too eager to give up their now-useless books, which were traded in for monetary compensation and were shipped off to the closest recycling plant. Six months later, the same deal was offered for families' gaming systems; an even larger number of donors showed up at the campaign's office (Kerry).

Hope's illustrious work as an activist proved to be a climatic shift toward an age of Truth-finding. Now no longer absorbed in others' stories and fantasies, society was given its first chance at self-actualization. In one of his yearly Motivational Addresses, Hope was one of the major world leaders who brought the key to unlocking human potential to light: "There is no need for writers and fable-tellers to feed you stories to yearn and wish for. Make your own wishes! But only if you can achieve them; for an unachievable wish leads to a dangerous path of self-absorption and unhappiness. . ." (Kerry). Science, math, and engineering met a new wave of popularity, and the trend continues to this day; Art and Music have both been added to the Dejected Degree list for most universities this past year to make room for more-refined majors in the sciences (Global Bureau of Miscellaneous Information).

Good Hope's influence was integral for society's success not only to achieve the Enlightenment of Truth, but also to help accomplish the complete eradication of Fantasy. "I thought it'd be good enough just to save us from Oblivion, and when I achieved that, I thought to myself, 'I can't stop there. I'd be committing a crime against humanity if I didn't finish the job to the end. I had to ensure this world's continued success and well-being," said Hope in one of his last interviews before his death (Kerry). Hope's activism holds effectiveness and inspiration to this day, saving billions from the peril that comes from Dreams that cannot come true. From the twenty-first century's perilous Second Renaissance to the twenty-third's New Age of Enlightenment to its continued Progressive Era, the line between Truth and Fantasy has always been fine; but because of the continued success of activist Good Hope, the world's society is now on Truth's side and is there to stay. From the eradication of religion and literature to the continued promotion of Realism (and the continued decimation of Dreams, for that matter), Good Hope is our real Savior; He is the one who has created the "Heaven on Earth" we live in today.

Gold Dust

ALEXANDRA GULDEN, Grade 11, Age 16. Lusher Charter School, New Orleans, LA. Brad Richard, *Educator*

I can count all the conversations I had with my husband. The first was not when we met, in an arranged meeting in 1911, which Telemaco spent "resting his eyes," as he mumbled it. My parents asked me what he was like, and I told them that he was nice, very courteous, and he would make a fine husband. I knew he would be the kind to leave me in peace, but this of course I did not say. In truth, Telemaco had been quite the desirable husband when our marriage was arranged. He had been, and when he died at fifty-three still was, handsome. His skin was like an Indian's, but his features were very much like a Spaniard's, sharp and regal. But his most notable feature was his green eyes, with which he stared directly and slightly uncomfortably at you as you spoke. The only reason he had not secured a wife until that point was likely due to his silence. The first time I heard him speak was upon our second meeting, eight years later. He had been reading a newspaper, but he did not give the impression of trying to hide behind it, and so I asked him how his college life in America had been.

"Good," he said jokingly, in English, and told me a little

bit about civil engineering, none of it comprehensible to me. I knew from my parents that he had been trained in building railroads, which with growing signs of foreign investment had seemed necessary, and would bring wealth and stability. But he did not discuss this with me. He quickly quieted, and I tried to rekindle our talk. At that time I viewed him as an armadillo, which simply needed some gentle prodding to unfurl itself. Leading him in conversations was almost the same as being the leading figure in our relationship. I asked him if he had read any poetry, Ruben Darío being my favorite, of course.

"I've only read textbooks and case studies in the last eight years," he told me. I asked him if he had any pictures of his travels. Without comment, he showed them to me. He only owned three: a portrait, a picture of him with the Latin American club, and one of the campus, which looked rather plain and chilly. I asked him about the temperature, and he said that it was quite cold but he hadn't minded, just pretended he was in the mountains. There was one thing neither I nor anyone else had wanted to ask him about, and that was the war. In our letters he had described things in such a detached manner that I felt as if I were reading a newspaper. At 2 p.m. it was announced that Nicaragua had declared war on Germany and the Austro-Hungarian Empire. With Guatemala, the Nicaraguan men of the Spanish and Latin American Clubs are to be drafted into the U.S. Army. Until further notice, their date of departure remains unknown.

As he was there for a little over a year, he kept track of what countries entered the war—Costa Rica, then Haiti, and Honduras—all tiny countries that could not lend much power, but by then the war was more or less decided, at least in my eyes. And Romania, Telemaco wrote with a hint of humor, had joined the war on July 10th, just the day before it officially ended. I don't know how much battle he saw, though I know he fought with the infantry in France. But I do know that he had the opportunity to be awarded as such and brushed it aside.

Like a fool, he fought for another country and came back home, brushing aside the citizenship they offered him. I don't know if he went into battle; he never spoke of it. During our second conversation, I asked him why he had turned down his U.S. citizenship for a less comfortable life.

He told me, "It is my job to build the railroads and to build prosperity for Nicaragua." I told him it must be nice to have a dream.

Now, when I am alone and have time to think, I think of money. I think of the money spent for his education on building railroads, the money wasted when he didn't build a life for us there, when we would all end up there anyway. By the time he arrived at his university, the canal had been chosen to be built in Panama, and as the water began to flow, so did all the wealth. Nothing would be left for Nicaragua, but at the time many chose to ignore this. If I marry him and he dies soon after, I had thought even at that time, nothing will be left for me here.

Our third conversation, on our fourth and final meeting before our wedding, was about money. "Telemaco, how much does it cost to go America?"

"I don't know."

"Why?"

"I did not pay for it."

"Who did, then?"

"A relative."

"Is he important?"

"Very."

On the night we were married, he turned to me and said,

"Maria Magdelena, we are going to live the rest of our lives together, so we must get along. Always try to ask me yes-or-no questions when speaking to me." I wanted to ask him why, and perhaps he knew that.

"I don't like to waste words," he told me. What a strange notion, I thought. What about words could be wasted? Perhaps the energy it took him to make the words—despite all those calculations he did each day, he really was a lazy man. And yet it seemed he was always writing a letter to someone, either for business or personal reasons. He was often away at the mine, and often I wondered how much he spoke, or how little. How did he conduct business meetings? And when I think of it, I never did ask what it was he did, if he owned it or ranked high. And so I never did know what it was that was stolen from me.

We spoke three times about matters of love.

Telemaco: Do you want to marry me? (Yes, it's already been decided.) Telemaco: I am a man of principle. (More on this later.) Telemaco: I love my daughters, but I hope this is a boy.

Aside from his silence, Telemaco had many odd habits, and without words to crowd them his actions stood out more starkly than they would have otherwise. He did not laugh often, and if one were to hear him it was easy to see why. He brayed like a donkey, his teeth (fine though they were) almost indecently exposed, and when something particularly amused him, he couldn't stop. But he had learned to smile with his eyes and never with his teeth. He lived like a mime, expressing himself to the fullest with expressions and hand movements, the nearest he could get to a silent life without learning sign language. But his system was so effective that I had forgotten the power words themselves could carry.

When I was carrying Juanito in my belly and the radio no longer blared songs but news of the second war, I asked

Telemaco if he loved me. *"Sí, te quiero,"* he said, like a child, a relative, or a man who does not want to sound too intimate. I want you.

"Am I your only woman?" I was not prepared for the answer.

"Maria Magdelena, I am a man of principle. Look at my friends who have five, ten, illegitimate sons. The only son I have is taking a nap in his room. There are many things in my heart: math, science, civil engineering, my family. While you may share space with those things, you will never share space with another woman. If you are dissatisfied, I will give you more space." I was too surprised to tell him no, I'm just fine, surprised to hear his voice stretched out over multiple sentences. Even the voice was surprised, rusty, as if it had not been used rigorously in a while. But I don't want it to seem as if he were always quiet. Oftentimes we asked each other little questions, about how the day was, or about little chores that needed to be done. Small talk, I suppose, although Telemaco loathed the term. Only once did he ever ask me a somewhat serious question, something unrelated to a grocery list or the laundry.

"Maria, you recall my age, correct?"

"Fifty-three, of course."

"And how old do I look?"

"Young, around thirty."

"Hmm." He seemed satisfied with this answer. I suppose he was somewhat vain too. Though I was seven years younger, I had begun to age more rapidly than him, my features softening and rounding. Gray had wound its way into my hair, and I kept it cropped short, like my daughters.

Though he wasn't around them much, our daughters were rather fond of Telemaco and followed him around the house. They thought me too strict and despised my company. Though they were girls, with them he played something that resembled baseball. Apparently he had played it at college and had missed it, but now it was beginning to become popular. Every Nicaraguan loves baseball, my son might have said, and so it had become by his time.

My son, my poor son, took after his father's interests but fortunately not his manner of speech. Like Telemaco, he was always off traveling somewhere and sending letters to me, until the accident over Honduras, in 1989. He was young, younger than Telemaco, but like his father he had still found the time to leave behind some daughters. .

Death only made Telemaco seem younger. And only on his deathbed did Telemaco talk for a longer period of time than he did about his principles. His summoned us to his side and told us about everything he would leave for us, what our futures would be like. His voice was raspy, like the hinges of a door gone to rust from lack of use and oil. I asked him if his relatives would intervene, and he was quiet. I don't remember a thing he said; everything sounded too technical and detached, like his letters. I don't suppose there was much value to it anyway. All I remember is the last word of it—gold. He was talking about the mines, probably describing Juanito's inheritance. Even then I doubted him; my old fears had never gone away. When his coughing seized and he looked peaceful, I had the maid guide the children away. The priest said prayers in the corner. He laid his hand on my stomach. How it kicks, his smile seemed to say. I took his hand and leaned close, listening carefully for a last word. Telemaco's lips puckered, painfully he whispered, "I have been saving my words for you, my love, for this moment. Remember that afternoon we talked?"

And despite the vagueness of his question I did remember, remember it still now, not with freshness but with a musty clarity, like that of a flower pressed against the pages of a book. It was an unusually cool day, like that of the mountains, and I had been sitting on the patio, mending the girls' socks. I had been unfortunately good at sewing since childhood, and I knew I could do a better job than the maid. He had been reading a newspaper, and, glancing at it, I noticed it was rather yellow.

"*Oye*, Telemaco, why are you reading that old rag?"

"Hmm, nothing much interesting, small town," he said, thumbing through the pages, and I noticed it was in French. "Take a look at the date," he told me, and so I left my work on the chair and leaned over.

"August 8, 1918," he said aloud, as if I was no longer there, as if the barrier between his mind and mouth had been undone.

"Nothing much interesting," he said, absentmindedly, as if commenting on the weather. How he hated talking about the weather.

"Except," he said, folding it carefully, "I died."

Brother

KEVIN HELOCK, Grade 12, Age 17. Ephrata High School, Ephrata, PA.
Cheryl Fritz, *Educator*

Brother. A brother. My brother.

A brother is like you, only taller, older, stronger. A brother is a lean, muscled figure, tall spear in hand, slowly shrinking toward the horizon and the little faded dot animals that mean food. A brother is lessons in fire, a pair of hands guiding your own in the firm but forceful striking of flint, the bright-orange sparks that spurt into the air and leave dull-green sparks in your eyes. A brother is laughing and rolling down the grassy slope, lying on your back and giggling and climbing up to roll down again. A brother is sitting in the tree on the top of the hill, swinging legs and pointing up at the shimmering lights watching you as you watch them through the black canvas of night over the world above. A brother is warmth in the dark, his blanket tucked over your shoulders as you sleep and he tends the fire. A brother is safety. A brother is laughter. A brother is love.

I am looking up at my brother. He is tall, and I must crane my neck to see his face. The sun peeks around his hair as he glances down at me, flashing a warm smile and patting my shoulder as we walk. We are at the bottom of the hill. I can see the flattened grass on its side where we roll down together, and I point eagerly, but Brother only smiles and ruffles my hair, indicating the fuzzy spots shifting and pacing in the distance. I look down at my feet in disappointment. Brother gives me a last smile, pointing to the tree before setting off toward the horizon.

I watch him for as long as I can; my day will be unbearably lifeless without him, and I must spend as much time as possible keeping my eyes on him to put off the inevitable task of occupying my own mind. My brother shrinks, reduced to a spot in the distance, obscured by the wavy heat coming off the grassy earth. When he has melted into the plains and become part of the land, I turn away, heaving a sigh as I set to my daily task once more.

I walk in circles about the hill, kicking at clods of dirt and little stones, occasionally raising my eyes to see how the vast, monotonous scenery of the flat horizon has rotated lazily with my motion around the single interesting feature in this expanse of swaying grass and stout shrubbery. Soon enough, it does not feel as though I am moving, but that the visible world is spinning slowly around, and I become bored again.

I march to the top of the hill and sprawl out under the shade of the tree, shifting my body this way and that to make myself comfortable. I fold my hands beneath my head and close my eyes, hoping to nap the day away in solitude, but I can still see the light of the sun burning through my eyelids. The shade provides no relief from the harsh rays above, and I give up on napping. It is too hot, and my skin is slick with sweat, though I have been lying still, willing myself to sleep for some time.

I stand, stretching my limbs and walking to the side of the hill, eyeing its steep slope almost hungrily. With the ghost of a smile, I lie on my side, throwing my weight sideways and sending myself tumbling down the hill. There is a momentary rush, but it does not last, and I am not laughing when I reach the bottom. Games are little fun when I am alone. I sigh deeply, attempting to brush away the yellowed grass on my skin, but it sticks in the sweat on my back and shoulders and limbs and all of me and makes me itch.

My mind picks out the single thing I have yet to do today, and my feet carry me with an excited step as I scratch idly at the grass. I part the tallest, lushest part of the grass and shrubbery, cooing in pleasure as my eyes find the little brook meandering across the plains. The water is shallow, barely reaching my waist at its deepest, but it is cool and refreshing against my skin. I sit down in its middle, the whole of me but my face and ears submerged in the fluid vein as my every muscle relaxes to drink in the coolness shade could not grant. My eyes follow the blades of grass as they, having parted from my skin, swirl circles about me on the surface before being whisked away downstream, some of them sinking from sight to settle on the bottom while others are hidden by the lazy arc of living grasses as they disappear around the bend.

I am overcome with a sense of luxury, enjoying every thrill of feeling as the water wakes sensations of shivery bliss from the outside of my body inward. I run my fingers through the water, studying the eddy and swirl of the liquid about me as my hands move through it. I bury my toes in the creek bottom before pulling away again, giggling at the sucking motion against my bare feet. I pluck at the grasses and reeds, throwing handfuls in the water to better observe the current.

It is some time before I notice that I am not alone. The hairs stand up on my neck as some primal instinct shouts its warning, and I turn my head with a frightened gasp toward the creature I know is watching me. I had enjoyed the feeling of the cool water, but now it feels like ice flowing into me from without, freezing my body into stillnes as I stare at the eyes watching me from the bank. My mind fills with images of a form pouncing heavily onto a body where it lies defenseless in the creek, and then blood running red at first and then pink as it clouds the water. I do not know where these images have come from, but they fill me with a wordless fear I have never known.

I stare at the creature, the bloody pictures sinking away from my mind as I pick out more details. The creature stands still, watching me with fascination too well defined to belong to an animal. It is taller than me and nearly as tall as Brother, and indeed looks very similar to the pair of us, though there are some anatomical differences I do not understand. Brother and I have short, fuzzy hair of a deep black; the waves cascading from this creature's head pass its shoulders and carry a lighter tint. I am puzzled by the swollen chest and the unfamiliarly pronounced width of the hips, among other distinctly confounding differences. I have never seen a creature like this before, but it is more beautiful than any I know. I do not know that it is called a girl.

The girl is the first to move. She takes a step toward me, and I scramble to my feet to prepare myself to run. My heart tells me that she cannot hurt me, but my head is yet unsatisfied. The girl withdraws the foot she has placed before her, frowning sadly at my hesitance. At once I am ashamed, and I approach her where she stands across the stream.

The bank is raised slightly where the stream has sunk itself into the soft earth of the grassland, and as I hop down into the water, my feet slap the surface and kick up a spray of water. The girl jumps as the water splashes over her, some of it reaching as high as her shoulders. For a moment, we are both frozen, and I am afraid. Then an unmistakable smile passes over her face, and she leaps into the stream beside me. In an instant, all caution is lost; we laugh together, kneeling in the water and cupping our hands forward to splash each other.

Soon we are lying on the bank, panting excitedly at our new-found friendship. The girl's hair is dripping and sticks to her skin, but she doesn't mind. We smile back and forth, and I delight in human company I usually lack on days like this one. I do not know where she has come from, and only vaguely understand that it must be from some new place I have never visited. My entire world consists of the hill and whatever can be seen from its top; that there could be anything beyond this is not a fact that has yet occurred to me.

When my breath has returned, I leap to my feet, parting the grass and waving an eager hand over my shoulder. My companion follows me happily, and together we climb the hill. The girl, having nothing of her own, coos in interest as her widened eyes catch on the array of possessions that litter the ground at the tree's base, but I, having already lain down at the edge of the grassy slope, tap her ankle impatiently. Then, as she watches, I hug my arms to my chest, close my eyes, and shift my weight until I am tumbling freely.

My stomach turns with my body's motion. There is a moment of sheer exhilaration as my lips part and a high note of euphoria escapes my throat, and then I am sitting up at the bottom of the hill, waving my hands in encouragement.

The girl is hesitant. She sits down and rocks her body from the knees, but her face tells me that she is nervous, as though the hill is some suspicious creature that will hurt her if she lets down her guard. Just when I think she will back away from the slope, she swings her knees a bit too far, carrying her balance with them. Her cry of surprise meets my ears as her hands grasp at air. Then she is rolling down the hill, her speed increasing with each revolution.

I am nervous. I think she may have hurt herself. But when she reaches me at the bottom of the hill, she explodes with laughter, her head thrown back and her beautiful eyes finding my own. Then she is up, and we are racing back to the hilltop.

* * *

It is some time later. The day is old now, and the sky has turned a dying orange as its eye burns itself up in approach of the horizon and night. After our play, the girl and I returned to the stream to wash off all the grass that stuck to our wet bodies. We stayed in the water for some time, passing time in the coolest place possible as the air burned outside. Tiring of this at last, we returned to the tree, and the girl went over my belongings with infinite fascination, turning each new trinket over in her fingers with wonderment as though it awakened some profound revelation inside her mind. When she had seen everything, we laid down on the side of the hill to nap the rest of the day away in leisure.

We are lying thus now. My eyes are closed, my face warmed by the now tolerable sun. I am aware of an agitation in the girl beside me, and then she stands quite suddenly. I open my eyes.

Brother is above me. He stands with his spear over one shoulder, a hunk of fresh meat skewered on its shaft. The girl is standing erect, her hands clasped nervously, her face solemn. Brother's face is the same, surprise having already left his features.

I jump to my feet, eager to introduce my new companion. I smile at Brother, indicating the girl with my hand. Brother's face twitches in a smile before his eyes return to the girl's, and I can see that he is pleased. The girl's face has changed too. She seems embarrassed and looks at her feet.

Soon the sky has darkened, and we are sitting around the fire. We eat the newly cooked meat in silence, a silence I do not like. Brother does not look at me. Instead, his eyes are fixed on the girl. She will not look at me, but casts shy glances at Brother.

My dinner is not enough to satisfy me. I want to laugh like Brother and I do when he is here. I want to laugh like the girl and I did when we found each other. I pick a fragment of bone from the meat in my hands, tossing it across the fire.

The bone bounces off Brother's knee, and he looks at me for the first time tonight. Only his face doesn't carry the smile I had hoped it would. Instead, my brother turns his eyes on me with a scowl of disapproval, as though our usual game has become childish. I have not seen my brother looking like this before. I am afraid and ashamed of myself, and I slink away from the fire to finish my dinner elsewhere.

* * *

It is night. I have finished my meal, but it is some time before I have mustered the courage to return to the hill. I am afraid that Brother will look at me like he did earlier, and so I approach cautiously. I keep my head low, crawling up the slope and listening for Brother.

The fire has burned low, and it takes me a few minutes to pick out the human shapes in the darkness. They are sitting in the tree, their feet swaying in the air beneath them. Their heads are raised to the heavens above, and Brother points with his finger, indicating patterns pricked in the night sky. Stargazing is one of my favorite things, and I am tempted to join them, but the memory of Brother's scowl is enough to make me reconsider. I stay hidden.

Brother is no longer looking at the sky. As I watch, he reaches beside him. The girl stiffens at his touch, but she does not vocalize her protest. Brother's hand lifts to her hair, and he takes some of it between his fingers, stroking it in silence. Then he lets go, reaching further than before.

Before I can begin to understand what is happening, a struggle has ensued. I see no detail, only the silhouettes shifting frenziedly in the tree. I want to stand, to call out to them and make them stop, but before I can move, a shrill scream pierces the night. One of the silhouettes falls from the bough, its voice cutting off as it crashes to the ground.

Brother and I are both frozen in the horrible stillness. Then he scampers down from the tree and bends over the limp form beneath him. A moment later, he is running off into the night, vanishing into the darkness.

When he is gone, I stand, hurrying to the girl's side. She does not move. She lies in a jumbled heap, and she is silent. I shake her, but she does not wake. Even in the dim light of the last glowing coals, I can make out the blood in her hair where her head struck the ground. I bend over her, listening for any sign of life, and at first I am certain that there are none. Then the slightest whisper of a breath reaches my ear. I relax, but only slightly. She is hurt.

I stare at the girl's immobile body. I shiver. Then my eyes find my brother's spear where it is propped against the side of the tree. At once, my whole body is convulsed with an uncontrollable shaking. Brother did this to the girl. I do not know why, but he has hurt her. There is blood in her hair. She will not wake.

Brother's scowl rises up from my mind until it is before me, filling my vision and turning red like the blood in the girl's hair. I am gripped by some animal passion. I leap to my feet, snatching up the spear before me and bolting off after Brother.

It is not long before I spot him. He did not expect to be pursued, and so he is not running anymore. Not until he sees me. I shout angrily at the sight of him, hefting the spear over my head. He starts violently, taking off in the opposite direction, but I have taken him by surprise, and the space between us is closing fast.

Brother crashes through the grass, and I hear his cry of surprise as he topples into the stream. In the dark, he has lost track of where he is. It is his last mistake.

I leap onto him, a murderous cry in my throat as I thrust the spear's point out before me. Brother gasps in pain. I can hear the crack of bone as the spear disappears into his back. My weight presses his head below the surface of the water. His limbs flail wildly, and I can feel his body shuddering through the spear, but I do not relent. I do not let him rise from the bottom of the stream.

When it is over, I leave the spear where it has lodged in his ribs. I stand on the bank, casting a last look at the water where it runs red and then pink and then clear. I start to lower my hands toward the stream to clean them, but they are already free of blood. I turn away, leaving Brother behind. I do not need him anymore.

In silence, I walk through the grasses and up the hill, at last finding myself beneath the tree. I pick up the blanket with automatic calmness, immediately setting about rekindling the fire. Then I sit in its glow, waiting for the girl to wake.

MATTHEW CRANFORD, *Ghoul in the Crowd*, Grade 12, Age 17, Atlantic Coast High School, Jacksonville, FL. Thom Buttner, *Educator*

In Eden

HENRY HICKS, Grade 11, Age 16. University School of Nashville, Nashville, TN. Dana Mayfield, *Educator*

Genesis 1:5

We buried Mama on the last Sunday of September, right after Bible study. I braided her chestnut hair and Papa put her in her favorite white dress and Emmanuel and Isaac dug a hole out back in the clearing. She's down there next to Judith and Beth and Grandpa. I'll be buried there one day.

"Esther, you'll live a long life," Papa tells me. "You'll be married to Emmanuel, and you'll have his children and when you go through the Changing, we'll send you off to Heaven too. Just like we did Mama."

Romans 8:5

We buried Mama on the last Sunday of September, right after Bible study. I braided her chestnut hair and Papa put her in her favorite white dress and Emmanuel and Isaac dug a hole out back in the clearing. She's down there next to Judith and Beth and Grandpa. I'll be buried there one day.

I want to be next to Mama when I go, but Papa's probably got it, and when Emmanuel has to bury him, I won't say anything.

I don't suppose it matters that much. "There's no need for our earthly remains," Grandpa told me when Grandma passed. Mama and me went three days without the men. "That's why we take the Long Hike. It's selfish to want to keep them close." Only when Grandpa died, Papa put him right in the clearing.

1 Corinthians 11:3

We buried Mama on the last Sunday of September, right after Bible study. I braided her chestnut hair and Papa put her in her favorite white dress and Emmanuel and Isaac dug a hole out back in the clearing. She's down there next to Judith and Beth and Grandpa. I'll be buried there one day.

We sent Mama to Heaven right after her Last Supper. We used the knives from the kitchen, and she smiled the whole time. After that, Papa took her to his room and shut the door. Isaac told me that he was lying with her, that he was committing the sin of the flesh, but that it wasn't really a sin, because she was his and "A woman belongs to her husband, body and soul."

Emmanuel can recite scripture. Although Papa's the only one who can see the book, Emmanuel is good to remember what we learn in Bible study. "And all of her earthly remains and belongings are to her husband."

Matthew 5:28

We buried Mama on the last Sunday of September, right after Bible study. I braided her chestnut hair and Papa put her in her favorite white dress and Emmanuel and Isaac dug a hole out back in the clearing. She's down there next to Judith and Beth and Grandpa. I'll be buried there one day.

Sometimes I think that I'd rather belong to Isaac. He's much kinder to me, but Papa says that Emmanuel will keep me in my place, which is more important.

Emmanuel is strong, and I can't have a husband who wouldn't be able to keep me safe, out here in the woods. After all, he is the firstborn.

Sometimes I find myself looking at the way Emmanuel's shirts seem to fit tighter than Isaac's, but I sewed them myself and I know that they're the same.

Sometimes I get this funny feeling in my stomach, and my hands get clammy when I bathe Emmanuel. I told Mama about this, and she told me it was lust. She gave me a whooping. I deserved it. Lust is with homosexuality and blasphemy. I try not to notice it anymore.

"God frowns upon you, girl," Mama said to me. "And you are to please him before yourself, always." Mama was a smart lady.

Ephesians 6:4

We buried Mama on the last Sunday of September, right after Bible study. I braided her chestnut hair and Papa put her in her favorite white dress and Emmanuel and Isaac dug a hole out back in the clearing. She's down there next to Judith and Beth and Grandpa. I'll be buried there one day.

And Papa and Emmanuel and I and Isaac—in that order—stood out in between the clearing and the house. Afterwards we went back inside and I got started on my First Supper and Emmanuel and Isaac stayed out to bury her. And Papa came over to me and I noticed that his shirt fit tight around his arms too.

And he told me that I was going to have to take up Mama's work; the cleaning, the cooking, the bathing. And I said: "Yes, Papa."

And he said that I was to marry Emmanuel in the winter. And I said: "Yes, Papa."

And he said that I was to have Emmanuel's son by the next winter. The first to live is always a son. And I said: "Yes, Papa."

And he said that I had a lot to learn about being a wife and mother. And I said: "Yes, Papa."

Isaiah 57:1-2

We buried Mama on the last Sunday of September, right after Bible study. I braided her chestnut hair and Papa put her in her favorite white dress and Emmanuel and Isaac dug a hole out back in the clearing. She's down there next to Judith and Beth and Grandpa. I'll be buried there one day.

Papa says that the first birth of a daughter is God's punishment for sin. He says that we must cut them down to show our loyalty to the Lord. That's why Judith and Beth are down there. We're not supposed to think of them, but they've got headcrosses too, so it's hard. I've named them—Papa and Mama didn't. I know it's silly, naming only a corpse, but I find myself wondering.

"What sin would they have committed to get a daughter?" I asked Emmanuel. "Mama must've committed the act of hedonism," he said.

"God frowns upon you, girl," Mama said to me. "And you are to please him before yourself, always."

"Why would she disappoint God like that?"

"Because women are weak, Esther."

Exodus 20:12

We buried Mama on the last Sunday of September, right after Bible study. I braided her chestnut hair and Papa put her in her favorite white dress and Emmanuel and Isaac dug a hole out back in the clearing. She's down there next to Judith and Beth and Grandpa. I'll be buried there one day.

On the first Sunday of October, Emmanuel and Isaac went to bed and I was left cleaning the kitchen after supper. I didn't see Papa until he was right behind me. He told me that I'm the woman of the house.

"Yes, Papa."

He told me that I was beautiful. He told me that I got Mama's beautiful brown eyes, but my yellow hair is his. He told me that I smelt nice, and I told him that Emmanuel never tells me I'm beautiful. He told me that it was a shame.

That night Papa confused me.

"I thought I belong to Emmanuel?" I asked.

" . . . and a woman belongs to her father, until he hands her off to a husband."

Luke 22:40

We buried Mama on the last Sunday of September, right after Bible study. I braided her chestnut hair and Papa put her in her favorite white dress and Emmanuel and Isaac dug a hole out back in the clearing. She's down there next to Judith and Beth and Grandpa. I'll be buried there one day.

Papa read from his Bible while Emanuel and Isaac lowered Mama's body into the pit, and I was there crying. He read about how a woman goes through the Changing when she's fulfilled her duty on Earth and has no more meaning. He read about how a woman belongs to her father, then her husband, then the Lord.

Papa's sits at the head of the table, always. Papa's the one with the book. He'll pass it on to Emanuel one day, but until then, it's only him who's meant to read it. He leaves it on the pedestal in the chapel.

"And lead us not into temptation," I remind myself. "But deliver us from evil. For thine is the kingdom, the power, and the glory. Forever. Amen."

Trial Period

NELLIE HILDEBRANDT, Grade 11, Age 17. South Carolina Governor's School for the Arts and Humanities, Greenville, SC. Alan Rossi, *Educator*

Cliff brought a girl home, an old friend from college, and I thought between the two of us, she was the one he would sleep with.

I made dinner for the three of us. She stood in the doorway while he sat on one of our yard-sale stools. I chopped baby bellas and covered them in oil, pushed them around a pan, and he played Dylan on one of our speakers. The two of them caught up on their new lives while I cooked in front of them, evidence of his. She had been studying art history when they knew each other in college, but now she was teaching English to high school freshmen. She was smaller than me, swaying in a long gray cardigan to "Pretty Saro," complimenting him on music we'd bought together.

"I love songs that are over five minutes long," she said.

She had a glass of the wine I'd bought with an employee discount, and Cliff and I had beer. He noticed how her hair had changed and touched a piece of it. "The red suits you better," he said. "I like how it looks when it's up too."

The two of them did dishes. He washed and she dried. He

let a glass slip, soap up to his elbows, and she laughed after it shattered. Pieces stuck in the mat in front of the sink. They stood still, exchanging smiles like parents telling their child an easy lie, while I swept the shards into a dustpan.

They sat in the dark on our back porch for a time. I turned on the light and they called to me, watery shouts through the screen door. I drank more so that I could look directly at her face. We watched lightning steep in clouds far away and saw it break the hills but heard nothing.

She told us about her artist's residency in Portugal and teaching in China for a year and going to grad school in Massachusetts. Cliff told her about our hikes in Appalachia, showed her pictures on his phone.

I didn't want to go back inside. They encouraged me to pee in the yard. We laughed as I tripped through the wet grass and turned up moss and peed under purple and black clouds, lit by lightning. Their laughing morphed into quiet talking as I crouched in a dark patch of lawn. I tried not to listen and to watch where I was stepping.

"We missed you," Cliff said. She was cross-legged on the arm of his chair, barefoot.

I touched my hair, pressed to my face with sweat. It felt for a moment like we were friends; that this was a home and we had opened it for her.

We didn't leave the porch after she left. White paint chips from the wooden rocking chairs stuck to our damp arms. We became increasingly sober. "Can you believe she's as old as me?" he said.

"She's nice," I said.

"Those pictures of Lisbon were beautiful," he said. He stared at the gnats floating around our porch light and wouldn't shut up after that. He told me he had planned a trip to Nepal with his roommate in college one winter when they were stuck off the interstate during a snowstorm. He said that they had sat in the car and filled a notebook with things they would need and things they knew and kept adding for months later.

"I wanted to go to Iceland," I said. "I had posters in high school, and books. Listened to all of the music." I felt like I was lying and I wasn't. "My friend works for a rental car company there now."

We were quiet.

"Let's go," I said, quickly, so that he wouldn't. "You can go do the Camino or whatever and sleep with your old college friends, and I'll quit my job and go to Iceland."

"The Himalayas," he said. "I don't want to leave you," he added.

We didn't bring it up at all that week.

* * *

I could feel myself needing to be closer. I pointed out movies that we had waited to come out to see and showed him pictures from our first dates, college juniors photographing each other in the abandoned house we'd found in the back roads, deteriorating rolltop desk behind him and unidentifiable food in the fridge. I reminded him of the bad haircuts we had given each other the night before we had moved south.

"Do you remember the first time you said you loved me?" I said.

He shook his head and told me that I was putting everything out in the open all of the time.

"It was in the Shenandoah Valley, in our tent," I said. "A man was playing the flute all night. You wouldn't let me leave to go to the bathroom unless you went with me."

"There was a drum circle outside," Cliff said. "Too many weirdos."

We had helped each other into visitor's centers with wet boots and practiced conjugating Spanish verbs in our tent at night, rain softening our voices, writing Foucault quotes and our names into the registers to feel resilient.

He always got sick to his stomach when he felt sad. He spent the night underneath the sheets and held his stomach and wouldn't let me touch him.

* * *

I smoked with the dishwashers who worked at the farm-to-fork restaurant I was hostessing in.

They were young and lived together. One of them kept weed in his gauges. I decided that I had nothing to lose. Thomas was twenty-three and the oldest dishwasher. He rode his bike to work every day and had a soft Southern voice and he told me something about me had changed when I came back to the restaurant the next week. I told him it was because I was going to Iceland.

"No, your hair is different," Thomas said. "Or your makeup or something."

"My boyfriend and I are taking a break," I said.

"You look cooler," he said.

"I'm quitting next week," I said. I didn't know what I was saying. "I'm going to buy plane tickets and then I'm leaving."

"Hang out with us before you leave," he said. "Tonight. To-morrow night."

"It's a Tuesday," I said.

Cliff called me, wondering when I would get off and if I had picked up bean sprouts from the supermarket. "We have a lot to talk about," he said.

Thomas sent me their address. I turned off my phone.

The train tracks went through their backyard. I could see people moving in smoke through their screen door. I didn't knock. A nude girl looked up at me when I walked in, not saying anything to anyone, not doing anything except looking.

I heard Thomas call my name. He wasn't in a white T-shirt and apron and black hat. I followed him to a small room where the dishwashers and more kitchen staff were sitting and passing around a bowl. I sat on the brown carpet and laughed at their jokes and they told me I was nice, and I didn't say that I hadn't done this since college.

"Frances is going to Iceland," he told the dishwashers. The dishwasher with the gauges passed me the bowl.

"Did you know that Iceland is the green one?" he said. "Greenland is the icy one. Have you ever heard that?"

"I have no idea what you're talking about," I said.

I woke up with four other people on a mattress that was half the size of the room and watched a small cockroach running up the file cabinet in front of me and returned missed calls from Cliff. He was crying and tired. I didn't want to come home then but I did. He told me he had been drinking and calling all night. I apologized. I threw up in the sink.

* * *

Cliff had a friend in Portland. He put the shirts I had seen every day for the past four years into a suitcase and away from me. We said that a break would be good for our personalities. I left him at airport security. I said that I would be in Iceland for a couple of months and rent out our house while I was gone, and we agreed that there was a reason that we'd been together for four years and that that reason would become clearer to us as we got to experience a few things on our own.

"Yes," he said. "I will see you very soon. We'll learn."

He sent me an email on the first night that I was alone. Attached was an image of him and his friend at a taxidermy-themed nightclub. They sat on stools next to a hyena, and he was holding a martini below the teeth. My stomach was warm like I was sitting with them.

My friend in Reykjavik sent me photos of a day-trip she had taken to a national park called Þingvellir, encouraging me to hurry and buy my plane ticket before the prices hiked too much. She stood in the rift valley of the Mid-Atlantic Ridge, where the Eurasian and North American plates meet. Next to her was dark, clear water and moss-covered rocks, no buildings or roads or telephone poles interrupting.

"You can walk along the crack in the plates," she wrote. "Pretty spectacular. Bring a good jacket and shorts. The weather changes every five minutes. Might want to practice putting up your tent in the rain."

I had a dream that I was looking for Cliff in the space between every continent. I hitchhiked between cities, and when the car door opened, he was behind the steering wheel. I told him my name and asked him where he was headed and he told me that he could drive anywhere.

* * *

My emails to him were about preparation.

I didn't talk about living alone or getting groceries for just one person. I debated buying a bus pass or hitchhiking the whole way around and whether or not I should wild camp and asked if he thought rice would be heavy on my back for a month. Each paycheck went into gear that I was unsure I would need—a Pocket Rocket and solar-powered phone charger and crampons and an ice pick and a small shovel. It sat in bags on the linoleum in the kitchen, waiting for me when I turned on the lights after my shift.

He wrote me back about a vegan strip club he went to and the new friends he had made and how he was writing a novella he had thought up while experimenting with mushrooms. His new friends liked to stay up late into the night and talk about things until light bled through the blinds and that it was just like college and that he was having some trouble getting into the swing of those types of things but kept busy.

"I bought a new tent," I wrote to him. "It's only two pounds and orange and has more room than our old one. It sent my bank account back into double digits—you don't want to know what flights are like to Keflavik right now. I'm going to pick up more shifts. I'll be leaving soon."

I worked for a couple of weeks and blew it all on things from REI that backpacking checklists on Iceland blogs told me I needed. A man with a ponytail fitted me with a child-size backpack because of my small shoulders and told me I would have enough room.

I put everything into the pack when I got home—sleeping bag in the bottom, socks into boots, dehydrated food into compressible bags, rolled clothing, Pocket Rocket and Swedish spork into a tin that I would decidedly eat everything out of, water bladder against my back, small shovel, first aid kit, flare and trekking poles and black flats into anywhere I could fit them, tent poles hanging out of the side pockets. The backpack wouldn't stand on its own. I could hear the water in the bladder gurgling within. I sat on the floor and pulled the straps over my shoulders, clasped the buckle above my hips, tightened. I couldn't get up from the floor. My knees didn't take the weight and I undid everything and pushed the pack onto the couch and tried to stand up with it from there. I walked around the kitchen with the thing on my back, then to the mirror.

There was nothing I knew I could sacrifice.

"When do you leave?" Thomas asked.

* * *

I sorted through menus at the hostess stand and threw out the stained or ripped ones. He was usually in the kitchen, but since he had acquired my phone number, he spent more time on the floor, talking to bartenders until he made his way to me. He spoke too loud to them after coming from the clatter in the kitchen, and I heard him say things like, "I think someone ordered a martini with dishwater," and the bartenders made him slice lemons while he looked at me, asking questions about my trip from behind the bar.

I told him I was leaving soon. That I just needed a couple of more paychecks and then I'd be out. I showed him the picture of Pingvellir. "It doesn't look very crowded," he said.

"It's Iceland—nobody lives there."

"Why would you want to go somewhere without people?"

"The landscape."

"What are you doing tomorrow?"

"I picked up a shift," I said.

"Come to the art museum with me," he said.

I needed the extra money but I wanted to be close to someone.

I sent Cliff a list of the things I was doing to get ready: three miles a day, one hundred pushups in the morning, fifty situps before work. Determining which dehydrated meals tasted the best by cooking them over a canister of butane, trekking up and down the stairs with my bag. Sometimes he said "awesome" and other times he said "I'm sure you're feeling really in shape" and sometimes he didn't say anything at all, not for days, and I would wonder where he was, and he would send me back a belated list of what he had done during the week—a marathon, couch-surfing within the city, a reading of his first chapter at an open mic, gaining respect of strangers—and I felt like I owed him something, like I needed to match his stories with my own.

* * *

Thomas had only ever ridden a bike to the restaurant. He was sitting in a wicker chair in his yard when I picked him up. We drank before the art museum. It was a small cement building, empty during the weekdays, an hour drive. Thomas tripped down the stairs, scraping his knees in the dark. Our laughter ran up and down all four floors.

I always ground my teeth when I looked at art. I was staring at the canvas and then the sides of my skull hurt. The paintings were too confrontational. I was tipsy.

Each floor was gray and the exhibits felt self-gratifying and cold.

We stared at a painting of a woman with no arms, sitting in a flower pot. I commented on how pretty it was but I didn't know why. "I want to be beautiful so bad," I said. "The poppies are supposed to be referencing opium, right?"

"Can I come home with you?" he said.

We set up my orange tent in my living room, filled it with my new sleeping bag and trekking poles and clothes in bags and stuffed all of those things toward the bottom to make room for our feet. We filled up on miso soup and tea out of tins and sat on oatmeal packets and bags of rice.

He timed me while I took it all down. "Again," he said.

I imagined that rain was flooding the linoleum. My nails were dirty and my hands shook from the cold and he started the timer and I set the tent back up, pulling the rain cover over the top and tying it to the stakes. The timer went off when I was still pulling the poles through the tabs.

"This is going to be a lot harder when it's been raining every day," he said.

"I'll send you postcards," I said.

I took him to my bed and tried to decide what to say while he sat on my pillows.

"Is your boyfriend doing okay?" he said.

"He's writing a novel and doing drugs," I said.

Everything looked different with him there. I shut the blinds and undressed and wrapped myself in a blanket and we sat in the dark, staring at the same wall. I realized I had accomplished what this break was for.

"How do I look?" I said. I gestured to my body. There was a pressure with these types of things and I would have to re-learn.

"You look like you'd rather be somewhere else," he said.

I pictured Reykjavik—dark blue pubs, clutching a Viking, dog-eared map in my back pocket, moss and rocks in a loop on the horizon—and how I would still be thinking of Cliff, running through Portland in the mornings, his reflection, reaching for him when I turned over in my sleeping bag and touched drops of water on the orange nylon instead, searching for a signal at the base of a glacier to maintain our correspondence, how I could hitchhike through Iceland for months and never feel like I had enough to tell him, endless daylight of the summer months urging me to stay awake and keep drinking and dancing with strangers, giving my name to the person sitting next to me on the bus, driving past waterfalls, white and hanging like string from the sides of fjords.

"You're wrong," I told him. "I like it right here."

ANASTASIA SANCHEZ, *Sullen Girl*, Grade 12, Age 17. Ramon C. Cortines School for the Visual and Performing Arts, Los Angeles, CA. Julie McManus and Oliver Shipley, *Educators*

Three Views on the Same Matter

DANIEL KALUS, Grade 8, Age 13. University School of the Lowcountry, Mount Pleasant, SC. Sara Peck, *Educator*

Emerico Prisco

"Why do I protest? Insecurity, scarcity, injustice, repression, deceit! For my future!" This is what signs read during the Venezuelan protests of 2014. Protesting was my way of saying that I wanted a better life; that I didn't want to live in the dumps.

I knew violence would come the minute police arrived on the scene. I started shouting for people to leave the streets and go back home before there would be tear gas and rubber bullets.

Nobody listened, so I and my friends rushed back to my small excuse of a house. We found beer bottles and gasoline in my father's grimy cellar. We stole alcohol from a nearby store. We mixed gasoline and alcohol and created about fifty Molotov cocktails.

We ran back to the location of the protests. Just as I had predicted, the police were shooting rubber bullets into the crowd and throwing tear gas at random. I took off my shirt and covered my mouth so I wouldn't breathe the gas.

We started passing around the cocktails and matches. I kept three cocktails for myself. I lit it with my match and threw it right at a group of police. When the other protesters saw this, they cheered and were encouraged to do the same. As for the police, most ran away from the cocktail except for one who was engulfed in frightening flames.

Alfonso Rosales

I sat down in the local police station when I heard about protests in San Cristobal, Venezuela. Our orders were to take care of the situation with as much force as needed. We were issued batons, police shields, and tear gas and rubber bullets to control the protests. The whole police force has never used these weapons before, outside of training. A fellow officer next to me trembled on the way to the site. We did not want to shoot at our fellow Venezuelans, especially because we held the same opinion as the protestors on the government.

Suddenly the car stopped, and our unit leader, Gustavo Abarbanel, shouted for us to move out. We made a line on the street so the protesters wouldn't get through. Why? I thought to myself as we stood there waiting for orders. Why can't we just have peace?

Gustavo Abarbanel

"Move out!" I yelled as my unit members rushed outside the car.

I take my job very seriously. I was born in a town called Silva in 1979, and I was raised to love the government and my country. I've always wanted to serve for my country. I joined the military at eighteen and haven't gone back home since. Today I am thirty-five. A month ago, a higher-ranking officer asked me if I could lead a police unit in San Cristobal as a temporary job. I agreed. I left the military camp in which I was stationed, in the outskirts of Puerto Cabello, for San Cristobal.

When I arrived, I noticed that the members of my unit were not taking their job seriously. Many were playing cards, some went to the bar, others were sleeping, and a few were watching TV. I marched into the damp room and yelled, "*Atención!*" The room went silent. All eyes turned to me. Suddenly, everyone burst out laughing. I was outraged. I took out my pistol and fired into the ceiling, after which everyone was silent.

"I will not tolerate this type of behavior in my unit!" I said. "I am your new Unit Officer. My name is Sergeant Abarbanel. You will always refer to me as sir, and someone fix the hole in the wall!"

Emerico Prisco

I was born and raised in a small neighborhood in San Cristobal. My mother is a veterinarian and my father is a cook. We own a small restaurant called "Comer es bien!" (To eat is good!) I came into this world in 1997. I was in high school when I heard some of the older students talk about protests. All I heard were the words *inflation, insecurity,* and *better future.* I sprinted up to them.

"I couldn't help overhear you speaking about protests," I said. One of the group members raised an eyebrow, "Yes?"

"Are you trying to start a protest, because if you are, I'm in!" I said.

The group smiled, and the one who spoke earlier said, "Great! We need everyone we can get."

Alfonso Rosales

I was born and raised in a city next to Caracas called Petare in 1986. My parents had family friends called the Bascos. They had a son my age named Hernando. I grew up with Hernando as if he were my brother. My family wasn't the wealthiest of the bunch; my father was a mechanic and my mother was a secretary in a textile factory. Hernando's father was also a mechanic and his mother a secretary.

Hernando and I soon grew up and moved to San Cristobal so we could find better jobs. We later lived in an apartment together because it would be cheaper. We joined the police force and were soon amongst the best officers in the unit.

Hernando and I were playing cards on the day our strict new Unit Officer came through the door. Unlike everyone else, Hernando and I didn't laugh when he asked for attention.

Gustavo Abarbanel
From that day on, my police unit became the best in all of Venezuela. I always attempted to be nice to Lieutenant Rosales and Lieutenant Basco. They were always serious and ready to perform their duties.

We were now in an armored van, and I was screaming for everyone to move out. Those protesters have no reason to protest. Our government is the greatest. I was in high spirits until I saw that Molotov flying toward Rosales, Basco, and a couple of other men.

Emerico Prisco
Since I met that group of kids, we've been planning the protests. I hated the government intensely. The people who worked for them were corrupt figures whom I didn't consider the least bit human. Well, that thought stayed there until I heard the screams of the officer at whom I threw the Molotov.

Alfonso Rosales

Hernando and I were trying to use the least bit of tear gas and rubber bullets. So far there wasn't too much violence. I suddenly saw a ball of fire hurtling toward us. I managed to get out of the way on time. Hernando wasn't so lucky. He was the only officer who got hit. He screamed and rolled on the ground. I dragged him back away from the scene behind a van and managed to put out the fire. His clothes were burned and he had big red spots all over his body. He went out cold. Sergeant Abarbanel saw us and rushed over.

Gustavo Abarbanel

I rushed over to Lieutenant Rosales, who was saying encouraging words to Basco, who was motionless on the ground. I took out my phone and dialed for an ambulance. I suddenly heard the sound of shuffling feet from a side street. I looked up. No one stood there. I went back to talking to the paramedics. I heard the noise again. This time I saw a young man who looked about sixteen or seventeen.

"*Hola*," I said.

Emerico Prisco

I felt that this isn't right. I'm not a murderer. I slipped away from the crowd and into a small side street to get behind the police. There were two officers huddling around the one I burned. One spoke on the phone while the other said soothing words to the one sprawled on the ground. I accidentally stepped on a leaf. The one on the phone looked up, but I ducked in time. I got up and tried to pass unnoticed. It didn't work. He looked surprised, but he then snapped out of it and said hello.

"*Hola*," I replied. I gulped. "I'm so sorry. I'm the one who did this." This caught him by surprise. The other one who was kneeling looked up at me. He had tears in his eyes. The other one hurriedly finished his phone call and said, "Elaborate!"

Alfonso Rosales

The kid told us his story. I looked sad, but the sergeant looked angry. "You are to be arrested at once!" he exclaimed.

"No! Please no," the boy pleaded.

"Yes!" the sergeant screamed back.

"He didn't know though," I said, siding with the kid.

"Know what?" the kid asked.

Gustavo Abarbanel

"You don't know that!" I replied. "He must have known. Why else would he have protested?"

"I don't know what you're talking about!" the kid yelled. "I was protesting because I'm not happy about our government. There is inflation, insecurity, and deceit. Now, can you please tell me what you were talking about?"

I was still suspicious, but I told him. "There was a conspiracy by Brazilian teenagers to overthrow the Venezuelan government. We are currently investigating anyone who knows about them."

Emerico Prisco

And so I explained to them about the movement toward a better government. I told them that the Brazilians were most likely not the only ones.

The ambulance soon arrived. The officer still suspicious about me went back to help calm the protests. The other one asked me if I wanted to come to the hospital with him and his friend, who was in pretty bad shape. I agreed.

"I'm Alfonso, what is your name?" asked the officer with whom I went. "I am Emerico," I replied.

We talked to each other about our past as the ambulance made its way to the hospital. He told me that the man I burned was called Hernando. Alfonso told me the story of his childhood; said he was practically Hernando's brother because they knew each other since they were born. The protests ended while Alfonso and I were at the hospital.

I swore to myself that from that moment on, I would never resort to violence again. Hernando eventually left the hospital but had scars that would never fade. After the protests, Alfonso and Hernando both left the police force. They finished college and became architects. I stayed friends with Alfonso, Hernando, and the sergeant, who I learned is called Gustavo. Gustavo stayed in the military and planned to remain until he was physically no longer able to. I made plans to finish high school, become an architect, and go into business with Alfonso and Hernando.

I was sad when I heard the bad news. Forty-one people died during the protests, and countless others were injured. Two friends of mine were killed when a Molotov cocktail blew up next to them. I remember that night. I wept like a baby. They died because they wanted change like so many others.

The Making of a Femme Fatale

LIZZY LEMIEUX, Grade 11, Age 17. Interlochen Arts Academy, Interlochen, MI. David Griffith, *Educator*

These are the rules of their mother's house: Don't smoke indoors, don't break ten o'clock curfew, don't come home smelling like a strange boy's cologne. All this, so the neighbors, in their matching white houses spread out over miles of green lawn, don't talk. Here comes Angelina like she's on a movie screen, breaking her mother's rules and flipping her hair over her shoulder with polished fingernails. Jesus, doesn't she know not to touch her mother with the same lips she kisses boys with, the same lips that open wide when she's parked under a billboard of the Marlboro man saying "You'll like it"?

Midnight came and went a long time ago, and until now her mother and baby sister have been sitting around the TV in the dark. The news lady is saying words like gang fights and dissatisfied teenagers. Their mother is saying words like damn kids and serves them right. Angelina leans down to leave a lipstick ring on her mother's cheek, her platinum hair falling over the two of them like a shroud. Only her roots remind her of her mother.

Then Angelina comes to rest on the couch opposite her baby

sister Carmela and flicks open a lighter. The sweat of her skin leaves marks on the leather. She likes how she stains everything her skin touches—leather, boys, they're all the same to her. Angelina's puckered mouth is aglow in the light of her burning cigarette.

Her mother watches the clock and smoothes down her little black dress. When she speaks, her voice is as sharp as her fake nails and collar bones. "One of these days," she says from her plush recliner, "all that hairspray's gonna go up in an electric blaze."

She'd like that, her mother. That way Angelina would get the halo her name implies she already has. That way Angelina would be high up with the angels, instead of being just plain high down here with the rest of them.

"How'd it go?" Carmela asks. She's wearing a silk nightgown. Nobody can see this, but sometimes it catches moonlight from the open bay window in the folds around her unformed hips and where her breasts will be and makes her skinniness shiny.

Angelina is shrouded in smoke. "I won," she says. She tugs the lip of her tank top down to expose more pale, pink skin.

"Yea? I bet you looked real good too." Carmela would bet everyone had their money on the girl dressed so sharp she wouldn't need a knife to cut someone. "What are you gonna do with the money?"

Angelina exhales. "Stick it under my pillow. Maybe I'll get my baby teeth back."

Their mother presses her lips together, says, "That's enough," and stands. The minute hand ticks to the half hour. She makes her way to the front door, high heels dull against the Persian rug. "Time for bed," she says, turning the knob and heading out. Her girls have grown too big for games. But she is a woman, so she can play with boys, even after hours.

The next morning their mother is MIA, gone from the manicured lawns and new-age manors, so she can kiss rich men when their wives are out. No part of their father has been seen in years, besides his signature on the fat child support checks. They've left their girls free to walk around the tiled kitchen with nothing but panties buckled around their hips.

"Carmela," Angelina says, looking her sister up and down, "you're flatter than a boy."

They drink orange juice straight from the carton and Angelina makes a cocktail by taking a swig of vodka after every gulp. This she calls a magic trick. Then she makes Carmela disappear so she can lounge around the living room with boys who have names like Marcos and Vito and their girlfriends who don't have names besides Baby.

It's mostly locals, Colts Neck kids, the kind who come from daddy's dollars and mother's disinterest, from McMansions invading farmland. These kids never stay long, just show up, get pie-eyed, spill their secrets and their drinks, go to fights in the city to get their kicks. Sometimes Mommy and Daddy call them stupid, and they're not wrong.

This is summertime as Carmela sees it. When their mother is making money, the boys and their Babies get high in the living room. When their mother comes home, Angelina goes out, showing up after curfew with a bloody lip and drunken smile, hanging off a boy like a playground tire swing.

Their mother does not worry about Angelina's bruises anymore. And even though she could tell all about the fights and the boys and the Babies, Carmela has learned to hold her tongue. Nobody wants to hear truth in the mouth of a twelve-year-old. But there's this girl, Virginia, and when Carmela speaks to her, the bolts in her jaw come loose. Carmela says Girl, this is the way it is, says, she's bigger than the both of us, says, we could become bigger if we wanted. Carmela speaks like a girl who knows and Virginia believes her.

Virginia is a neighborhood girl, and some of the older boys like to ask her around to their place on Friday nights because she's got it. Carmela asks her around to her place sometimes too, because she wants what Virginia's got; she wants Virginia. She wants to be able to sink into her curves like a pair of jeans, but she'll settle for running her hands over them instead.

One day, Carmela and Virginia sit at the top of the staircase, which hangs over the living room, and watch as Angelina and the boys and the Babies make a ring out of their bodies. In the middle there are brightly colored bottles that leak onto the white carpet. Voices bounce around the emptiness of the vaulted ceiling, and Carmela and Virginia hear everything as an echo. Below them, the boys have their hair slicked back, newly cleaned knives weighing in their pockets. When they crack jokes, the Babies giggle with their hands so close to their mouths they look like they're licking the dirt under their long, polished fingernails.

"You were real good last night," says Some Boy to Angelina. "Son of a bitch didn't even get a chance to swing before you took him out. Aren't I right?" He nudges another one of the boys who's busy kissing a bruise into another Baby's neck. "Huh? Aren't I right?"

"Your girl's a real dish," the other one manages before his tongue finds its way back to the hollows of his Baby's throat.

Another time, the two of them, Carmela and Virginia, sit and sun themselves by the pool that is cut into the backyard. They spread out beach towels on the concrete and pretend to be older than they are by chewing on the ends of candy cigarettes.

"They'll make you one of theirs," says Carmela. "One of their

Babies. You'd look good, all made up, so maybe you want that."

Virginia blows a puff of sugar into the air. It falls back and powders her dark hair white. "Maybe."

"I guess I don't, but that's since nobody would have me. Everybody wants Angelina, since she can fight them and kiss them too, and that makes her different. But nobody would think of having her baby sister."

Virginia closes her eyes, and her lashes stick to her pale cheeks. "Mela," she sighs, "somebody wants to have you. I just know it."

"You think I'd be better off a boy?" Carmela asks. She will never be Angelina, with her smoke ring halo, slitting people with her pocket knife and polished nails, but if she were a boy, she'd put a knife in her pocket and kiss girl's throats. Then nobody would say she wasn't pretty, because she'd be pretty good at cutting.

"Maybe."

Sunshine beats against Carmela's smile. If she were a boy and this was a movie, she'd play the heartthrob and Virginia, the heroine. They'd say I love you instead of I love that dress. She closes her eyes. "Me too," she says.

* * *

When Carmela cuts her hair, Virginia sweeps up the split ends. When she bleaches it and red-raw burns show up on her scalp, Virginia soothes her, slow and sweet. Last week, they heard a boy tell his Baby she was real good, meaning his girl was real good at making people bloody.

The two of them sit on the edge of the clawfoot tub and stare into the mirror.

Virginia leans her head on Carmela's shoulder. "Now that you're a boy, I look just like your Baby."

"I'm not a boy," Carmela says. But maybe she's enough of one to lean over and suck meaning out of Virginia's mouth. Maybe she's enough of one to find the kind of meaning that boys pick out of her sister's teeth. Maybe she's enough of one that a knife will appear in her pocket like an appendage.

Underneath the door creeps pot smoke and voices. They are saying things like "Dress sharp" and "Get a move on." The front door slams with the sound of a bullet. Through the slatted blinds, Carmela catches her sister in split pieces, sees Angelina staring at her wavy reflection, sees Angelina climb inside Some Boy's car and kiss Some Boy hard, sees Angelina careen out of the cul-de-sac and out into the flats of the free-way.

"Wonder where they're going," Virginia says.

Carmela, because she's a girl who knows, sees another split piece of her sister in her head; Angelina is in the back lot of a diner. Everybody is placing bets on her because she's string-ing them along with her mile-long legs. They're putting money down on the fact that Angelina is not just one of the boys. She's better than that.

"I don't." Carmela stands, runs her fingers through her chop-py hair, and frowns into the mirror. "Come on," she says to Virginia.

* * *

Joy-riding, Carmela calls it, as if it's all about a game, about taking the scenic route. They're going too fast down the free-way to the only place in the whole world that's open until mid-night, where teenagers are fighting with fists and knives and who knows what else. Damn kids are gonna get themselves killed.

"What are we gonna do when we get there?" asks Virginia.

Carmela's knuckles go white, and there's this ache from wanting to hold Virginia instead of the steering wheel. "Didn't anybody tell you we're going to a fight?" she asks. Virginia shivers. "I mean, I got. I was just thinking that we don't know how to fight is all. The boys know how to fight."

"Fuck the boys," Carmela says. "That's how it used to be. But, well, Angelina's gonna set that straight. And we're gonna be there. Don't you get that?"

Everybody knows Virginia's got it, so she laughs. "Sure I do, Mela. You're going to a fight because you think it's in your genes. Maybe because your sister has the knowhow, or maybe you think since you cut your hair you can cut somebody. I get it, Mela."

"That's not what this is!" This is what this is: a way to . . .

Carmela steps harder on the gas and hits the steering with the flat of her hand and a strand of blond hair falls into her face.

Because Virginia is afraid of seeing the inside of a body bag, she pushes the strand of Carmela's hair aside with her pink fingernails. Because she is afraid of seeing a world without Carmela, she lets her fingers linger. One of those things is worse than the other, but Virginia is not sure which.

Above them, billboards that Angelina gives blowjobs under rocket by, saying things like Livewire and They Last. It starts out as nothing but stitched-together farmland and big, empty houses and blurs to suburbia, hung to dry on the washing line of the freeway. Everything is black until they rush through a tunnel and their bodies are bathed in honey.

This is how it goes for miles. This is how it goes until the city cuts into the sky like a blade, until there is a diner with drunks on bar stools and neon signs on walls and a parking lot filled with used cars. Carmela lets the car skid, tires squealing and leaving streaks of rubber behind them, until it comes to a stop over painted yellow lines.

"You ready to see what it's all about?" she asks, pushing open her door. The screams, of Angelina inside a circle of boys pumping their arms and girls twirling their hair, are soft.

"We shouldn't be here," says Virginia. She knows some of the boys in that crowd, and they turn to look at her. This time they aren't staring at her chest or hips. In the dark, she gropes for Carmela's fingers and their hands melt together with the heat of their shame.

"Don't be a baby," says Carmela. "I'm your Baby," says Virginia.

This would make Carmela laugh if she wasn't so lightheaded.

They walk the thirty feet between them and Angelina slowly, and the hush becomes a whine becomes a roar. Up close, the gang smells of aftershave, shampoo, and sweat. Carmela licks her lips while Virginia stands on tiptoe.

"I can't see," she says.

With her elbow, Carmela pushes the crowd aside until there's a gap like in Virginia's front teeth. The two girls fit themselves into it and watch Angelina fighting a boy, a city kid, wearing a leather jacket and cuffed jeans.

Angelina's ass is hanging out of her leather mini skirt. Her stilettos are on the sidelines and her orange nail polish is chipping where her big toe is cracked all the way up the middle, deep as her cleavage. She's taking a swing at the boy and hitting him square in the mouth. They turn golden in the light of a streetlamp, almost cherubic. When the boy coughs up blood into Angelina's face, they look like fountain figures, spitting spring water onto the pool of yellow-lit concrete.

"Your sister is hot stuff," says Virginia.

Carmela shrugs. "Maybe," she says. Her eyes catch on all of Angelina's curves. "That boy is so dead."

There are mosquitoes feasting on Carmela's arms, and she

does not bat them away. She just grins. "Maybe," she says.

Virginia is leaning forward. When she starts to scream her shouts stand out, high-pitched and childish against the low roar of everything else.

Angelina's eyes dart sideways and hook on Carmela and Virginia. She watches them move as a unit, bodies bending under each others force. The boy aims a kick into Angelina's stomach and it lands, because she is staring at her little sister and her little girl lover. Angelina cannot breathe. Angelina's eyes go big. Angelina's mouth matches. Angelina is saying something, and it sounds like Stop! Nobody hears.

She falls back with each blow of the boy's fist. Her head makes a dull noise on the pavement and splits. Then, the boy digs something shiny into Angelina's stomach. Honking cars in the city and late night news in the suburbs and whining feral cats in heat back home are all screaming Stop!

Carmela's fingertips are fuzzy. Her head is hazy. The word *fight* and the word *stop* get so jumbled up that she feels her tongue aching and heavy. Every time her sister stumbles backwards, Carmela pulls Virginia into her. Soon, everything is numb besides the places that touch Virginia's pink skin. Her fingers feel like exposed electrical wires.

Carmela watches Angelina's red blood run against yellow lines of parking spaces and thinks: Angelina is sharp. Angelina is slick. Angelina is hot stuff. Angelina is not a chalk outline of a body, not a statistic, not midnight news, not morning news, not somebody's sob story.

She tries to pull her up but her hands are shaking, says her sister's name over and over in her head. Angelina, Angelina, Angelina. This makes her sound like her mother, which makes her scared.

The boy backs away, leaving Angelina with a knife in her side and cleaved skull. The night is hot and dry and cloudless. Money changes hands. There's screaming and headlights and Some Boy drives away with another Baby in the hook of his arm.

"Mela," whines Virginia, "do something."

So Carmela kneels down at her sister's side and thinks about cupping all the blood and funneling it back into her sister. "I can't," she says.

They say that dying is about going into the light, but Angelina is already there. She's lying in streetlamp puddles and the shine of the moon. She has nowhere to go, so she's got to live.

Virginia leaves Carmela while she strokes Angelina's baby-soft blond hair. Blood's matted into her bangs. There's an ambulance wailing in the distance but Carmela is too busy trying to soak up her sister with her shirt and saying Angelina's name to hear. The night is singing in sirens and Angelina's.

They take her away on a stretcher. They say, "Who can we call?" And Carmela says, "She's got no one who cares."

"What's going to happen to her?" she asks. And they say, "Maybe she'll live."

Virginia forces Carmela into the driver's seat. "Step on it," she says. "We shouldn't be here." They streak toward the mouth of the tunnel and its bitter, yellow light.

"Your mother will want to know where her girl is," says Virginia.

Carmela shakes her head. "This is the way it is. To my mother, all this, it's just a news story."

Behind them, the diner is the size of a dime. They pass suburbs with sleeping sisters, farms with animals waiting for a butcher's knife. Everything is Angelina. Everything is Some Boy's Baby. The sun is coming up, and everything is bleeding out.

The War

MELANIE MENKITI, Grade 8, Age 14. The Village School, Houston, TX.
Donna Pilgrim, *Educator*

Cousin Ngozi has always been a man of few words.

My parents always told me stories of how, as a baby, Ngozi would never utter a word unless he was hungry. If his diaper was full, the house girl wouldn't notice, for it wouldn't smell until hours later. If he had to burp, he would hold it in his mouth until he fell asleep—then, he would leave the nursery with a repugnant odor that only a baby could make. He wouldn't speak unless spoken to, and barely had any friends as a child. When he turned eight, he finally managed to speak by himself. His first words were ones that haunted Auntie Adanna for years: "Daddy is dead." Uncle Gerard died of poisoning from the dirty water in Onitsha. Ever since his death, Ngozi has worked relentlessly in the army to make Nigeria a better place, something Auntie Adanna strongly disagreed with. "We're not Nigerians," she often said in her native tongue, Yoruba. "We're Biafrans. Nigerians don't accept us." And while I never understood it at the time, now that I am fourteen and caught in the middle of one of the most catastrophic events possible, I comprehend it fully.

That is why when we receive the news that Cousin Ngozi is dead, on September 1, 1967, I am not surprised. We are currently at war with Nigeria, we Biafrans, for we want to be a separate country because of our conflicting beliefs. I've always known this day would come. It is inevitable in war; death is everywhere.

Auntie Adanna cries out multiple words in Yoruba that I don't understand—Igbo is the language I've always grown up knowing, despite pidgin English being my first language. Yoruba belongs to a different tribe. But my mother, with her gele-wrapped hair and wet, dark eyes, rushes to hug her sister-in-law, her lanky arms struggling to reach around Adanna's wide back. *"Ndo, ndo, ndo,"* she repeats in Igbo. Sorry, sorry, sorry.

I follow mother's lead and rub her back soothingly, chanting the same apology almost meaninglessly. I want to tell her that she had to have known it would come, but I can't. Mother seems to sense my frustration and sends me away. *"Anya mgbeumu,"* she whispers in my ear. *Take care of the children.*

I live in a house, unlike most of my schoolmates. My father works in the army; our lives are not as hard as that of many Biafrans as a result. However, because of my grandmother's strange obsession with creating dozens of offspring, almost every member of my family lives with us. Auntie Adanna, Uncle Oluchi, Auntie Iris, Auntie Ebele, my father, Auntie Fumnanya (despite her being barely an adult; we consider her our cousin), and all their children. Along with my mother, the house can often be *mkp?chi. Stuffy.*

When I enter the house, the sounds of an argument echoes from the kitchen. I follow the noise; Chidimma, my twelve-year-old cousin, clenches her fists as she glares at her mother, Auntie Ebele. Fumnanya sits at the dining table, staring on with mild amusement in her dark eyes.

"What happened?" I ask. They both halt and turn to me; Fumnanya glances up, but her eyes dart elsewhere immediately. "I'm in trouble," Chidimma sighs.

"And for what, Chidimma?" Auntie Ebele asks. Her voice is monotonous, but I can feel the vexation oozing off of her.

"I called Fumnanya an *ashawo*, and she tattled."

Fumnanya shifts uncomfortably in her seat at this comment. I furrow my eyebrows; Fumnanya is anything but that, and how did Chidimma find out about how she gets her food from the relief center?

Unfortunately, at that moment, my younger cousin Nnamdi decides to wander into the kitchen just in time to hear Chidimma swear. "What's an *ashawo*?" he asks innocently. It almost makes me giggle, looking at his wide, curious eyes. "An *ashawo* is what Fumnanya is. A slut."

"*Chidimma!*"

Auntie Ebele's shriek of agitation shuts Chidimma right up. The twelve-year-old stumbles past me and out of the kitchen, clearly upset. "Chika," Auntie says, getting my attention. "She found out through some rumors running around the town that the priests are sleeping with girls. Fumnanya was crying, and she . . ." She snaps her fingers, as though trying to find the right words to say. "*Jikotara nt?p?.*" *Connected the dots.*

I lean down and gently hug Fumnanya. Her hot tears burn my cheek, and her snot ruins my flimsy T-shirt, but I don't say anything. Fumnanya never gets back until late, but each time she holds a bag full of food. She sacrifices the most sacred part of her body—daily—for us to have food. Fumnanya is not an *ashawo*, she is brave. "*Na ? na- d?kwa mma,*" I whisper. *You're alright.*

"*Ndo,*" she whispers as I leave the kitchen. "About Ngozi."

Upstairs, it seems as though almost no one is remorseful

about Ngozi. The younger cousins are running around, shriek-ing, while the ones slightly younger than me are simply playing cards. It's sickening. Don't they understand a family member just died? I want to scream at them, to hurt them until they realize the severity of the situation.

It is then that I sink down to the floor, my throat constrict-ing as tears threaten to spill from my eyes. I can't. I can't cry. Not yet. My body seems to disagree, for as soon as someone lays a gentle hand on my shoulder, I burst into tears. Horrible, revolting shudders and shrieks emit from my small frame, my fat lips curl into a hideous grimace, and I can't see—the tears are making my vision far too watery. I look disgusting.

"Chika, it's OK," I hear Uzoma, my five-year-old cousin, whisper in my ear. My stomach churns; Uzoma shouldn't be telling me that it's OK! Her mother, Auntie Iris, a half-caste woman, is out of the country because she can't return to the war. Her father, Uncle Oluchi, is suffering from depression since the war started, and often drinks himself into a deep slumber. Uzoma is the one who is in the most pain—why am I allowing myself to be taken care of, when I must take care of them?!

Ngozi has always taken care of me, and yet I can't do this simple task. At fourteen years old, I'm already a failure.

MIA STANTON, *Lungs*, Grade 9, Age 15, Pittsburgh CAPA 6–12,
A Creative and Performing Arts Magnet, Pittsburgh, PA.
Heather White, *Educator*

Abril

VASANTHA SAMBAMURTI, Grade 12, Age 17. Charleston County School of the Arts, North Charleston, SC. Danielle DeTiberus, *Educator*

Gael

Whether the universe thought so or not, I was a magician. I had coaxed quarters from the outer ears of my friends, and felt doves strum my skin before taking off from the cage of my palm. I still felt them sometimes when the buttons of the lights burned beneath my skin like live coals or exhausted eyes.

Red. Peach. Ocher. Blue. I could blend lights of any color with the stage as my palette. Monday nights featured Rafael's mariachi band, doing covers of Vargas de Tecalitlán, with their sombreros slung low. Tuesdays and Wednesdays were stand-up, and not particularly good stand-up. But Jorge wasn't picky about his entertainment, and neither were his customers. Rich or poor, bright or phlegmatic, they all sipped the same tall drinks and showed their teeth whenever the curtains split like a smile, and out popped the next performer.

But there was no other day like Friday. Friday, when cocktails were discounted by ten percent, when Abril kept you company.

Abril. She was every woman and every man, but at the club

she was a woman, always. That was, until the curtains zippered up and she slipped out of her dress. She undressed herself all she was, and it was then that she became the man I saw on the corners of sidewalks, wig tucked under his arm like a pet, his walk graceless. But the glitter always stuck to his skin like moss.

Jorge nodded at me. I pressed a button, and down came a spotlight, like a celestial answer. He mumbled into the microphone, "Testing, one, two." He skirted his eyes across the audience, seeming peeved by the divisive sounds of their conversations but aware of the tips they would leave later. He cleared his throat. "Consider it your luck to know her, your misfortune to not. Bonita, bonita, my special friend. Our north star, Abril."

And from the direction of his hand, out she sprung. I rolled the spotlight to her as I had done many nights, but I could never soothe the twist in my lungs that came with seeing her. The fruit of her mouth, the hollows of her cheeks, the cosmos in her eyes. So blue, those eyes. The straps of her dress were as thin as a breath. She lifted her arms, and they sank into her shoulders.

"It's another glorious night in Acapulco." She brought her gaze down. "Need I ask if you missed me as much as I missed you?" A cheer rumbled from the audience; she smiled. "I knew it. *Como te voy a olvidar*?" She spun a small paper fan in her hand. She opened it like a deck of cards and fluttered her eyelashes. "How will I forget you?" That was my cue. The controls slid beneath my fingers like beads on an abacus. It was hard work, perfecting these frequencies. But, when Los Angeles Azules's *"Como te voy a olvidar"* floated through the speakers, I knew the magic had just begun. This was a new song for Abril, but she was no less enchanting than she usually was. She allowed herself to be lulled into a trance beneath the layers of music. Rich brown hair running over her shoulders like water over stones. The paper fan held high above her head, as she rolled her hips and sent a fat kiss to the audience. Such empathic yelps of delight. I could see how alive she was. I switched on the red light and watched it dye her skin. "*Amor, amor, amor,*" she started singing. I softened the light. The red carnations that had bled like vines over her face paled to an ephemeral pink. She spun. I sent her a beam of gold. The color ricocheted off the sequins of her dress, glittering like the scales of a fish.

Abril pulled the feathered boa from her neck and slyly sidled up to a male patron in the front row. He had a feigned look of embarrassment as she garlanded him with the boa and let the fabric play about his neck. He fed her two dollars, right in the mouth. Light studded her teeth, the line of her cleavage was cut deeper. I mixed the lights from gold to fuchsia, to orange and lime. With each shade, she grew, as if inhabited by the light.

Abril was bold. Bold in the shimmying curves of her body, bold in the ecstasy on her face, and the cacophony she created. She was an art that I had embellished, and she barely knew my name.

Barely.

"*Mira*, Luis?" I heard an older woman say, nudging her husband. He was sitting glumly, sliding the ice from his drink in lethargic circles. He looked up at her touch and she pointed to the stage. "Her face. So pale."

He shook his head. "Just the light."

Gray. Violet. An electric blue. Her face grew paler every time, but she still danced like a comet. The energy of the music contrasted with the stillness, the sickness in her eyes. It just took a sliver of forest green, for her hand to clutch her mouth, to barricade her stomach trying to punch its way out through her lips. But it happened. The music was so loud you couldn't hear her retch. But you could see her insides abandon her—a soupy mess of no specific color. The peso floating in it. Staining her fingers, fogging the reflective sequins on her dress. Someone groaned. There was a stench. From the Abril whom I wished was my own.

I cut the light to black. She ran. I stood up.

A feather, that was all that was left.

Juan-Carlos

Here she was. The famous Abril. Her mascara drawn into crow's feet, her eyelashes sticking to the lids like cliffhangers. I pried them off. There was a smog of lipstick mixed with vomit. On my chin, the base of my neck, the corner of my cheek. Even in the wig.

I had no choice but to take it off, and I felt a strand of myself separate as I did. I couldn't explain it. With her hair in my hands, Abril was dead. I had killed her. All that stood before the mirror was me. Juan-Carlos. A scrawny man with a bald cap, in drag.

In drag, in art. In the fabric of myself that God had not stitched me with. But I didn't resent Him too much for it. He had given me Abril. And even for those fleeting moments on the stage of the club, she could erase me. That is all I needed.

I pressed a wipe to my neck and trailed up, wiping all the vomit off, regaining some of what I had lost. Trashed it. Worked the next wipe into the charcoaled crevices of my eye. That's the only thing Abril and I had in common. My blue eyes.

Blue like the coast of Acapulco, blue like blood unwed to air, blue like Mama's swollen cheek, wed to my father's knuckles.

Some say it was the alcohol, some say it was the job, but I say it was a lack of love. My mama's and father's parents used to joke about getting their kids married, until they actually did. It took seven seconds before she said, "I do." Five before his wedding band left a mark on her collarbone, before her ring tarnished his chin. They stayed in Acapulco for their honeymoon, blood rose like a clenched fist in the eyes of my father, blood stained the flowered sheets of their suite.

I wasn't an accident. I was the shell you expect the tide to spit when it rolls back to shore. There was a poetry in that. But it took the affection of my mother, and the silence of my imaginary friend to recognize it.

My friend had no name, no gender. They were just a soft presence that I could always feel, always turn to. When my father snuffed out the last candle on my birthday cake, I felt their translucent fingers clasp my eyes. Protecting me. I was twelve. Later that night, we went on a walk down to the beach, just the two of us. I kicked a spray of sand and wished those candles had absorbed him, my father, just as a lamp swallows a genie. Instead the grains just seeded my eyelashes, and I felt the soft fingers of my friend wiping them away, in the form of wind. *No.* They said. *No anger.*

Slow and ruminative. *Dance with me,* my friend said. "How can I? I can't even see you." I sensed a shrug. *You lead.* There was no one around. My face was wet with mist. I self-consciously swayed from side to side on my feet. My parents danced, but never together. My father's movements were as rough as his mind. But my mother, she was fluid. She was strong. She danced less like gossamer, more like a spider's web. I thought of that. I spun. I beat my feet into the sand. *Your mother's hair is beautiful.* "I know." I remembered the way it pooled over her shoulders as she rolled her arms and snapped her fingers. I longed to experience that too. *You can.* But how? There was a net of seaweed a few feet from us. They pushed me toward it. *Go on.* This is embarrassing. *There is no one here.* This is strange. They pushed my hands toward the seaweed. Maybe at that point, it was just me. I tentatively placed it on the crown of my head. It was thick and wet and I felt like crying. I couldn't do this. *There is no one here.* I moved my arms as my mother did; the seaweed, it dripped on my shirt. *You're doing great.* I circled around myself to mimic the movements of a dress. I bit my lips to make them red. Fierce.

This coast will be my home. I can dance however much I want. I can steal cake. How absurd. How freeing.

I couldn't admit to myself that I was scared. About someone coming, someone seeing me. The worst would be my father. For solace, for peace, I thought of goldfish and horses without reins. I thought of papayas, lime juice, and sand dollars. I thought of my mother's hair, both dark and strong, a fulfilled promise. I imagined the way it hung in long ropes around her face, like the tree swing in my Abuelita's house, which, just the previous summer, had propelled me to the stars in a continuous half-moon motion.

I tricked myself into thinking I had long, shiny hair. I toed the ground in avoidance of the skittish crabs that shot around me. There was no more music. I think my friend had fled. But they left the silhouette of someone new in my mind, a new facet of myself. I danced and danced. An odd string of jacaranda blossoms lay limp in the water, like a jellyfish. Even then, I had a knack for symbolism. I named this part of myself Abril.

My mother never liked the smell of jacaranda. She would spray her freshener when I brought the buds home. But I always awaited the springtime, and I always loved them.

Abril

It was spring that I walked down the San Francisco streets and saw a small cluster of artists file one by one into a nightclub. Bearing the stature of what I perceived as male, hair sewn in an elaborate trellis, their mouths and eyes painted like ceramic vases. One of them took a wrong step in their heels but was caught by a friend. The two laughed together. I remembered the deep tenor of it. My mother took me to get ice cream that very moment. The shop was in the opposite direction.

Times had changed, and she knew Abril existed. But she treated her like the shadow of me, Juan-Carlos. A *débilucho*, a wimp. I didn't like to think about that word too much.

Though it could swing open freely, there was a knock at the door. "Abril?" The voice was hesitant. It was a man's voice, but I couldn't quite place his face. I didn't feel like answering, but the knocking persisted, more aggressively. "Abril? Tell me. What's wrong?"

"Stomach bug," I lied. "At least, I think so." I faked a cough. "Yes, that's it."

"Do you need anything? I'm worried about you."

My hand paused at my left brow. "Why? Do you know me?"

"Not as well as I'd like." There was a breathiness in that.

"Who are you?"

A pause. "No one. I'm just here."

I held my breath, listening for the scuffle of footsteps or the release of a breath that would at least provide some insight, some quirk I could attach to a familiar face. Nothing came.

"I appreciate that."

"It's the decent thing to do."

"You needn't concern yourself with it. All artists are mortal." I held on to the sink. "These things happen." A pause.

"Well. If you need me, I'm here."

"I'll remember."

He left. It took me three counts to bring my face to the mirror again. But once I did, I was reduced to who I really was.

My face looked like a wound. The last remnants of makeup had stained the cloth in my hand. I stared and stared at this imposter, at myself. At the gray lips now spare without the rounded flourish of lipstick. At the cheeks more gaunt than sculpted, once the bronzer had been removed. At the eyes, now shriveled, like the filament of a broken lightbulb.

I could wear the most lavish clothing and blend my makeup. I could sing like Ana Gabriel. But at the end of the day, I would always be like this. Plain and afraid.

Behind me, a toilet flushed and a woman exited the stall. She washed her hands. On the way out, she glanced at me briefly. "Just so you know, men's is around the corner." She left.

I turned the hot water on to the highest setting I could. The mirror began to fog. Erasing the man no one wanted to see, matching the oceanic mist I would always behold. Fierce.

Ana

Marcos had given me them for our third anniversary; shining red pumps. They were too big. The more closely I looked at them, the more garish they became. I should've thrown them away when I got the chance. Now they hung from my son's feet like shackles—he had broken them.

"What am I supposed to do about it? You're the one who likes to dance."

"Nothing. I just wanted to show you." He tucked his leg beneath the chair once more. "I'll fix it tomorrow. I have nothing to hide."

He downed the rest of the glass quickly. The rings beneath his eyes were so deep. *Mi hijo*.

"Get some rest." I placed my hand on his head, but I felt the hair beneath it slide. I pulled away. "It makes me sad, to see you this way."

"Then don't look." He got up. "I'm sorry, I'm getting glitter on everything."

"I bought new soap yesterday."

He rubbed his temples. "I'm too tired to scrub it off."

"Try. It gets on everything."

He unclasped the heels from his feet and kept them beneath the table. There were red sores on his skin. "Good night." He said. I waited until I heard the click of his door to take his seat. The apples were starting to brown. I ate one of them.

What can I do? He had warm blankets and fresh apples. I boiled his water, and he wore my lipstick. What more did he want?

There was no difference between my son and a disco ball. He couldn't take a good picture. He never stood still. He shone for everyone but me. I finished two more apple slices. My stomach hurt and my foot hit something.

The red pumps.

Juan-Carlos used glue all the time for school projects. But now that he was out of school, there was no use for it. There was still an old tube in the kitchen cabinet. I went and got it and looked at it for a long time. His fingerprints were still preserved in dried glue. I unscrewed the top and let it spill on the base of the heel. I was too tired to be doing this. But I hated seeing broken things.

The heel adhered to the shoe once more. I replaced it in the same position it had been, in the same uneven angle. It was a quarter till eleven. I still wanted a cigarette. But, maybe now, I could finally rest.

There was one apple slice left. I finished it.

In the Summer, My Brother

JULIA WALTON, Grade 11, Age 16. Academy of Notre Dame de Namur, Villanova, PA. Norma DaCrema, *Educator*

At lunch our dog walks into the kitchen and eats my brother's fruit and then leaves. My brother feeds it to our dog himself. When our dog is done, my brother wipes thick spit from his hands and says our dog needs lunch more than he does. I say, But Brother, I cut that fruit for you.

To slice an apple, hold the apple with its stem facing upright. Position your knife slightly away from the stem and slice downward to the cutting board. Do this on all sides of the apple. To make smaller slices, position the apple face-down and chop to any size desired. Give your brother the apple core. He will suck off the excess meat to get you your money's worth.

In the summer my brother plays soccer and baseball and hockey with a half-dozen neighborhood kids and an ever-present symphony of cicadas. Though heat presses in from all sides—I keep our kitchen stocked with three fans for some relief—my brother plays Horse until his shirt is soaked through and he smells like our dog. He goes out in the morning and plays until lunch; at lunch he comes into the kitchen and he eats his fruit.

At lunch I ask, "Why do you play so long out there?" I peel the skin off an orange. He sighs. "It's better than being here all the time."

In my heart of hearts, I do not blame him.

They play in the field behind our row of houses, a sunbaked field of grass between one neighborhood street and the next. The grass is brittle and scratches my brother's legs and pokes his soft flesh when he falls. At lunch he has pear-green bruises. My mother would have done something about these bruises, but she is at work too much to notice.

Some neighbor had put nets there. My father had provided two moveable hoops. The kids produce their own balls and bats and pucks—my neighbor's son has no hockey stick, and my brother gives him our own.

"Why couldn't you have just let him borrow it?" I ask as I place a fresh bowl of blueberries before him. He shrugs. "It's what dad would have done."

Later that summer, my brother punches my neighbor's son in the face.

To cut a pineapple, place the pineapple on its side, and with a sharp chef's knife, remove both the crown and the stem of the fruit. Place the pineapple upright, and begin removing the spiny outer skin. Be sure to follow the pineapple's contours instead of chopping straight down—this will result in the most possible meat. The brown eye spots must be removed; cut a V-shaped groove along the diagonal line and discard each set of spots. Lay the skinned pineapple on its side again—cut into ring-slices—cut the ring-slices into chunks.

Feed the pineapple to your brother. He will be disgusted. It will be too sweet, and it will coat his tongue with bumps he can't get rid of.

At breakfast my brother will not talk to me. I wake him up

at seven after my mother leaves for work, and he rolls over and rises slowly. He sits at the table and rubs his eyes and grunts at things I say; he yawns and doesn't say himself much of anything. He eats oatmeal with brown sugar and bananas. He finishes. He leaves.

It is seven forty-five. The neighborhood kids will not begin to arrive until nine, and until then he plays basketball by himself. I can hear him through the window as I wash dishes at the kitchen sink: the ball falls dully on dry grass, sharply on rims, swishes slightly as it leaves his hands. The clock ticks slowly behind me. I turn off the water, and I listen some more.

In mid-July my brother comes in for lunch and he speaks. I pop cool grapes into my mouth. I ask him, "Why just play games every day?"

He props up his head with his hand.

"I don't need to talk much when I'm playing soccer, or baseball, or whatever. I say what I need to, and then I just do it. It's all about the game. I don't need to do anything else."

"Do you really hate talking that much?"

"Yeah," he says, "guess so."

I think, you didn't used to.

I think, you used to sit with me on the porch in late afternoon and eat lemon water-ice from the grocery store, and you'd tell me play-by-play how you won your baseball game, ground ball to left field to get that last runner in. I'd say, what, not a home run? You would laugh and say, well, you can't win them all like that. Our dog would sit by your lap, and our mother would wash the dishes, and our father would return from work to eat lemon water-ice too.

My brother finishes. He leaves. The kitchen is empty.

My father had a silver hockey stick, and loved conversation, and hated cranberries. He gave my brother extra chewing gum and played catch with my brother every night until dark.

In the summer, days stretch on into infinity. To my brother there is nothing to expect before or to remember behind. There is only a pickup game in a field of low-cut grass and sunlight. There are people around him, most of the time; there are people who do not ask and people he never tells. He holds himself steady. In his mind he can lose himself by kicking a ball toward a goal again and again and again.

To dice a papaya, lay the papaya on its side and chop off the top end. Slice the papaya lengthwise—it will smell funny to your brother, who cannot quite put words to any sensation. He will say the inside looks like a cantaloupe, besides the smooth black seeds. You will disagree a little bit—you've dealt with enough fruits this past year—then you will change your mind and say, well, you guess it does after all. Hold the half-papaya firmly in one hand and scoop the seeds and sticky membrane into the trashcan. You will be absentminded, and forget there is no bag. Clean the trashcan. Put in a new bag. Your brother will help you. Slice the halves into halves, saw each section's skin off, and dice the whole thing until your arms start to burn.

Eat the whole thing with your brother. He will have never tasted papaya before, but he will eat it.

My brother runs races with the neighbors' kids and after lunch I leave the kitchen to go and watch. It is hotter out there without my three fans. The grass is sharp. It tickles my feet over my flip-flops. The kids make a line with baseball bats and hockey sticks and they lean down as the oldest says ready-set-go. I can see beads of sweat on my brother's face—on his forehead, on the tip of his nose, on the line of his upper lip; his freckles seem darker than they once did. His brow furrows deep, and as they sprint away, his face holds the same expression.

Near the soccer-net, a boy bumps into my brother.

"What the heck?" says my brother. He is angry. His brow sinks lower and he gets in the kid's face, and the kid is the neighbor's son who now owns our hockey stick. "Look, it was an accident, OK? You were right in front of me!"

My brother scoffs. "You think anyone's gonna believe that?"

My neighbor's son boils. His chest puffs in indignation. His eyes open wider ever so slightly, and his mouth presses together in a thin line. "Look, you don't get to be a baby just because your dad died!"

My brother stands stock still for a moment, just a moment. Then he recoils, and he punches my neighbor's son in the face.

There is anarchy, for a little while. Other kids have to pull my brother and my neighbor's son apart. My brother wipes away a stream of blood from his nose and stalks away. He walks past me. I turn to him. He avoids my eyes. He leaves.

To open up the heart of your brother, wait until just before twilight. As you're chopping tomatoes for dinner, he will return from the day's sport and sit at the table and cry. Finally, he will cry. He will take a deep breath, at first, then wrinkle his nose; the bottom of his lip will tremble, and he will cover his eyes with fists like a child. He is a child, as he has been all this time. He will wheeze. He will breathe hard and fast. His whole body will shake, and you will place down your kitchen knife and you will hold him.

Say to him, Brother, it's hard to live beneath thick citrus skin. Let me peel away your problems upon my cutting board; I will chop up your loneliness and lay it there on the kitchen table. I can't swallow it whole, Brother—I must do it piece by piece.

He will say to you, I miss him. Oh, God, I miss him. To your brother you will say, I know.

To your brother you will say, I miss you more.

Lila

VIDHISHA MAHESH, Grade 10, Age 15. Folsom High School, Folsom, CA. Kacie Shingara, *Educator*

i.

Lila's mother tells to me that the loneliest people keep coming to her photocopy shop. She says it with her smile of yellow teeth, as heat fingered her copper coil skin. Lila's mother has many statements in her head like this, and she says them to people unguarded, as though she is dispensing lollies to little children. It is a manner of hers.

I ask her, "How do you know?"

To which she answers, "I know from their smell."

"They have a smell?"

"Yes, they do."

She says, "My father had the same smell, that's how I know."

"Was he lonely too?"

"He was deaf mute. Probably was."

"What do they smell like, these people?"

"That is too many questions."

"Just one more?"

"Now it is two."

You could never extract lollies from Lila's mother. You had

to wait for her to give them to you, as part of the private game she played. I had to wait until the next day, because she had begun to turn off the computer and her cashier and all the big breathing machines. She had stopped looking at me, and I let go of one breath. This is how she says it is time you go home. Lila's mother did not like to say these kinds of things, so she hoped that you would listen to the silence and understand.

I say, "Bye."

To which she replies, "Bye."

I walk out of the photocopy shop just as the neon light spelling OPEN flickers then spoils. A man with a beard and cuffed sleeves hurries past me, and though I do not turn to look, I wonder if he is the lonely man. I wish that he had slowed so I could smell his special smell.

In front of me the road swells like an eating giant, concrete fabric stretching over its stomach. It is a walk uphill from now on. The sun is setting very slowly as it does every day, waiting for someone to notice it. No one notices it.

Lila's mother lived in the small room above her print store, amongst little piles of photographs that had been ordered but never collected. Lila's mother lived with grim men, lived with toothless children, lived with happy dogs and sad girls. Lived with cracked families, dead families. Sometimes in the afternoons she would dust their faces. Sit with them for tea.

Lila's mother collects people. Collects strangers. Says she doesn't like to throw these kinds of things away.

I take a path in between two houses and feel the pebbles pushing against my sole because the path is not paved. It is another five minutes, so I allow myself to think. I think about my hillie billie father, and how he is not like Lila's mother. My hillie billie father (self-described) bought a house at the end of a crummy unpaved road that went through a gathering of trees, spending much of his money on it, and tonight he is preparing ramen noodles for both of us to eat.

I think of how the veins on his legs are visible, and how they grip the inside of his skin like pond weed. I think of how his voice has been broken into many pieces, and how his words contain echoes of his previous words, and how we do not talk much. In our house he brews silence until it boils over and runs stale. My father hasn't been working a while now, we have been nibbling from dying savings, but there is no bee sting in this town for that kind of business. The thieves have come through every window in this hill town and have stolen, unnoticed. Here each wife is secretly a spinster, husbands do not drink but neither do they live. Mothers weep every morning, a gentle raining, for things they do not have.

Like children.

On banging the door shut and then saying hello to no answer back, I walk to my room and shut another door. I sit at my desk with nothing to do, and look at the yellow-dotted town beyond my window. First there is a barricade of trees, then the lights begin to gather like a lake. I can hear the brook and its shivering water. I cannot see it, I can only hear it. So I hear it. I listen to its night greeting, the quiet howling that makes itself elegant. I listen to thrumming gulps, how it swallows the sound of street dogs crying, the nightbirds talking, insects vibrating. I listen to the other things that it has swallowed, other voices, small sweet voices that it has swallowed. I listen and I think of how it did it unintentionally, but with no apology.

ii.

The only story my father told me was about the little girl who went for a walk with the street dogs. It is an ancient story in town, even though part of the story is still alive and breathing amidst it. It is the only story that did not shiver because of my father's broken voice. It stayed in my ear like a whistle.

The story begins with a little girl who came home from school one day and decided to go for a walk with her street dog friends. She did not come back. I was a young seed when it took place, so I bear no recollection. My father told it to me like a fairy tale. Sitting on the chairs of the living room and listening to radio news, he turned to me and said, "Remember that girl."

I looked at him.

He said, "Don't try to be too brave."

He said, "I saw her from my window. I was the last to see her."

I asked him, "Didn't you tell anyone?"

He said, "I am tired now."

His voice was weak and silence stretched thin like a rubber band. He did not look at me but instead went to the porch and sat on his chair. He took out a cigarette and lit it with a matchstick, which fell to burn with the other dead ones on the ground. He was thinking of his past life, as he did every night on his chair. He was thinking of the songs his voice was too thin for, he was thinking of the times he could have made himself big but didn't. He was thinking of past loves and present loves. He was drawing comparisons. What he had then and what he has now. He was thinking about firm assessments, on the staying and on the fleeting. On the stillness and the moving. On topics that he could no longer touch.

He wasn't thinking of me.

iii.

A girl came home from school one day and decided to go on a walk with her street dog friends. She never came back.

Sometimes I hear this story at school. I say, "It is very tragic."

iv.

When I enter the photocopy shop, there is the beard-and-cuffed-sleeve man at the cash counter. I pick up a marker from the box and pretend to have money to buy it as I stand behind him in line, because I want to smell his smell and know for sure that Lila's mother is not lying.

When he is out of the shop, Lila's mother turns to me and says, "You smelt it, didn't you?"

I say truthfully, "No."

She says, "It's alright. You are not as old as I am, so it is harder for you."

She smiles at me and I see her yellow teeth against plum pink lipstick. I sit down on the stool, listen as she clicks dully at the computer. The fan rotates and whips the heat around. Time passes through the furniture in clouds of evaporating dust. Soon Lila's mother begins to turn off the computer, and the big machines all slowly die, and I get off my stool and stretch.

When I reach the door and turn around to say bye, Lila's mother says to me, "I smell it on you too."

Her hair is crinkled where it is parted at the center. She smiles her yellow smile, and I see the holes in her teeth. Dead and crying teeth holes housing people and their ghosts. People who have left her, now living in her teeth.

Lila's mother has put down all the lollies she has to offer today. I retire my questions, look at her and I smile.

I do not say to her, "I smell it on you too."

She does not say to me, "It is time you go home."

We do not say these things to each other.

v.

They tell me later of how the body was found, in the early morning of magical blues and magical clouds. They say it was cold as a fish, thin hair strands came away with touch.

On the descent of night time it had begun its shrinking. Eyes open, fully aware. It had been lain on the street on coarse fabric, the watchers were silent dots, and it was talking to the moon. Thin smoke of communication went between them, suckling at all sound. They tell me how previously the sun had gone up then gone down, how it had set but no one noticed. They tell me how she sat next to the little dead girl, eyes wet but not with tears, searching for where the blood had left its skin, left it dry.

Copper coil and the fish. They spent the whole night talking.

vi.

When I reach the house, my father is asleep on the old sofa. I go to my desk and sit at it. I look at the spotted town, and I locate Lila's mothers spot, and I look at it. I listen. I hear the brook singing its song. It is talking numbers tonight, marking calendar dates. Noticing the patterns of years.

vii.

My father tells me that mothers are very important for children. My father tells me, fathers can never be mothers. But I think he is just making an excuse.

The Proper Life

ADRIANA WATKINS, Grade 12, Age 17. St. Thomas More Academy, Raleigh, NC. Franz Klein, *Educator*

Foster's bones were quaking even before he pulled onto Broad Street. For the first time in four years, he was watching the snow drift onto the roofs of his hometown, and he was arrested by guilt and nostalgia. It was in that paralyzing minute that he rolled through the stop sign and onto the main avenue.

Broad Street was everyone's place of nightmares; even the most hardened drivers took extensive measures to avoid it. Thirty years ago it had been labeled a "historic street," meaning that it contained numerous potholes of varying sizes, and that every effort to repave it could be instantly stonewalled. Unfortunately, the only good businesses in the town existed there, and so it was both the most-trafficked and least-liked place within fifty miles. It was no surprise that the music of downtown Ericsville was a spectrum of profanity drifting from driver's-side windows.

Most citizens were used to the perils of Broad Street, and braced themselves before making the fateful turn. Foster forgot to brace himself. At the first dip he was launched six inches above his seat, out of his thoughts, and over his regret. He came down with a thud that left his teeth resonating in his gums and his heart in the other side of his chest. A succession of other potholes followed; when he was a child, his mother would exclaim, "An earthquake in Ericsville, New Hampshire!"

Amongst Foster's rattling thoughts—home again, home again.

Halfway down Broad Street he made a sharp right and proceeded slowly, for here it was: his neighborhood, redrawn in snow, just the way he'd pictured it on many nights in his apartment. It was only mid-morning now, and the Christmas lights were off; still, Foster saw them and smiled. He preferred those of the city, but these would do for his poetic visit home.

His house was the eighth one in the row. When he got to the sixth, he let off the gas and leaned on the brakes, and his immaculate car groveled up the street like a criminal before the jury. A sedan was in the driveway—his brother must be home. Suddenly, Foster's holiday plans were war strategy.

Five minutes, he thought, five minutes and I could be gone like I'd never come back.

But two hundred miles just to back out? He tapped the brakes again and a pen went rolling across the dashboard; an idea went rolling through his head. He may not be brave enough to talk to his brother face-to-face, but while he was in town, he might as well leave a note. The Christmas gift of an apology! There—he was a good Samaritan again. He grinned in earnest as he tore a blank page from his address book and began to write.

Mr. Beckley Goodwill,

Merry Christmas! Joyful greetings to you and your wife (if you have one) and your children (if you are so unfortunate). I offer you my sincere wishes that these last four years have been happy, prosperous, and filled with blessings; it is commonly acknowledged by all that you deserve them. Here's to hoping that the memory of our beloved Mrs. Jane Goodwill has been well preserved in your house . . .

Foster's pen lagged somewhat.

—Here's also to the apology that ought to've taken place several Christmases ago. This party deeply regrets his actions and begs your seasonal mercy on his faults. He will also be returning shortly to his adoptive home; a statement of your forgiveness may be sent to the following address . . .

Here he scribbled the number and street of his New York apartment, slurring a letter here and there in the subconscious hope that perhaps, after all, his brother might not contact him. After this, he signed his name in flourishing script.

—F. T. Goodwill

Then he put the car in park, bounded up the porch steps, and slipped the note through the mail slot with a satisfied sigh. Briefly, he stood admiring how well the old place had weathered the past few years, and what a job Beckley'd done in keeping up with the maintenance. Maybe the childhood memories softened him, because he thought briefly, After all, it might not've been so bad to see the man . . .

It was then that the door opened; Foster's hopes betrayed him and he jumped. When he dared to look at the person's face, he did not see Beckley, no matter how he stared. The glassy-eyed old woman on the threshold was a complete stranger.

"Excuse me," she said. "Are you from the postal service?"

"No, ma'am," said Foster.

"Oh," said the lady. "Then I don't suppose you could give this to them for me? This note dropped through my door a moment ago, and I'm afraid it doesn't have the proper postage. That's an offense, you know."

"I'm sorry," said Foster. "That's mine. I left it for someone, but there must be some mistake. Do you know Mr. Goodwill?"

"Beckley? Yes, yes, a wonderful man. Aren't you lucky to know him too! I could talk for an hour about what a wonderful man he is."

"I'm sure. But, by any chance, is he home?"

"Oh, I couldn't say. He lives down on Beech Street now."

"Beech Street?"

"Yes, he moved there after he sold me the house."

"Sold it!"

"Your hearing must be as bad as mine, bless you. But yes, he sold it, and for such a nice price after I talked to him about my husband. A wonderful man, Mr. Beckley Goodwill—I'll say that til I die."

Foster had wrapped a gloved hand around the porch railing. "Yes, well, thank you," he said. "I'll be going now."

She handed him his note and he left in a hurry. On the drive back to Broad Street, he kept thinking, Sold it! Sold the house! Sold our mother's house! How hard had their mother worked for every floorboard of that place? Was there any price high enough for the living room where he and Beckley had learned to read? And whose was it to sell?

A thousand such thoughts wound Foster's fingers tight on the steering wheel. Before he knew it, he'd bumped his way to the end of Broad Street, where he parked in the slush and took refuge in the restaurant on the corner.

There must've been a strange look on his face, because the hostess gave him a seat in the far back, facing the wall. Foster propped the menu up and scowled at the daily specials. Half-way through their list of pancake flavors, he felt he was struck with the answer to everything. Revenge! he thought. That's got to be it. That's what this is about, in the end. Revenge!

Perhaps it was too easy an answer. And perhaps it wasn't

very much like Beckley to hold grudges. But what else could it be? The only other plausible reason was that perhaps Beckley hadn't wanted to live there anymore—preposterous! He had even more wonderful memories of that house than Foster did. It had to be revenge. There was simply no better explanation.

Foster was just picturing Beckley's nefarious plot when a sunken, manicured hand reached over the top of his menu and dragged it down from his face. Then, as unexpectedly as there'd been the old woman at the door, there was a pair of familiar eyes in front of him.

"Ruthie!" he cried. "What a wonderful surprise!"

The girl dropped her hands in her lap; she was smiling, but more from obligation than sincerity. "I saw the hair and thought it looked familiar," she said. "And, well—look at you! I was right."

"Of course you were. You're always right."

"You flatter me, but you know that's not true. I bet money years ago that you'd be home for Christmas, and I wasn't right then, was I?"

"Sure you were! I am back for Christmas."

She gave him another marionette smile. "You may be a few too late, Foster. Oh, but look at you," she said again.

The bell on the counter rang, and Ruthie stood up immediately. It was then that Foster realized she was wearing the restaurant uniform.

"You still work here?" he asked. "But you'd always planned to be long gone by now."

"Oh, that was years ago," she said. "Now, I have to get back to my shift."

"Already? We've hardly caught up! Please, Ruthie, sit down. I can't let you go so soon—you were practically a sister to us."

"Of course we'll talk more, don't be silly. Come back around three and I'll be off."

As she started away, Foster called after her, "Don't you want to know if I've seen Beckley?"

This last sad smile was the only earnest one in the group. "If you'd been to see him, you'd've gone to the bar," she said.

Foster spent the next four hours avoiding Beech Street; as usual, Ruthie had changed his mind.

As he walked, he looked on the town as he never had before. He felt all the buildings around him were only dollhouses—plastic, saccharine, and devoid of content. The townspeople, too, seemed juvenile, all of them ignorant children under Foster's gaze. And yet he knew they'd always been this way. It was only he who had changed, by the saving grace of city light.

Thank you, he thought. I'm no Pinocchio anymore.

Finally, the time came to meet with Ruthie. She was already waiting with two cups of coffee in the corner booth.

They drank in silence until she spoke.

"So, tell me, why come back now?"

"I guess it was just the right time."

"Why not earlier?"

"I guess I wasn't ready."

"You're doing a lot of guessing. You sure?"

"Of course I am. It's the truth, Ruthie—I had a lot to sort through, you know. After Mom died, I had no idea what to do."

"And I understand. I've been counseling your brother, you know. But Foster . . ." she sighed. "You left, just like that. It was your mom one day and you the next, and no warning for either of you. You should've called."

"Maybe, but I panicked."

"So did we." She leaned closer, and the coffee was deep on her breath. "But do you want to know something about Beckley? He's told me what his worst day was. And it wasn't your mom's stroke, and it wasn't when you disappeared; it was the day after that, when you were still gone. Because up until then, he thought you'd come back—and you didn't."

"Why should I have?" Foster snapped. "I got along just fine in the city, better than fine. I hate to hurt Beckley, but he can handle things on his own."

"Don't tell me that about anyone who's lost their mother," said Ruthie. "Especially not Beckley."

She stood up to leave. "I do a good job of being his friend, but I'm not his brother. That was your job. I think you should ask yourself why exactly you didn't come home to do it."

"Where are you going?"

"I've got errands to run, and you'd do better to think than talk. When you're ready, your brother's on Beech Street now—it's the house with your mom's Christmas lights. You won't miss it."

She was gone before he could tell her he'd changed his mind. There would be no extended visit to Beech Street for him; no need to reopen old wounds. He would simply leave his note at Beckley's house, like he'd wanted to do.

Even so, he found himself morbidly satisfied with his brother's misery. Perhaps he'd mattered more to his family than he'd thought.

With the note tucked in his coat pocket, he began to walk. Around him the store windows were dressed with displays: here, coats; there, china like his mother's. What had become of that china? He supposed Beckley had sold that too. If it'd gone to Foster when she died, it would be stowed away safely, but he hadn't stayed for the division of property. Besides, she would've left it to Beckley; he'd been her favorite by a hair. Of course, that certainly wasn't because Beckley had been the better student. And Foster had been a bit more musical, more dedicated; he'd persevered with trumpet lessons when Beckley had quit after a year. Yet, by some inconceivable logic, Beckley was still the one who was doted on, the one who had the glimmering future! He and Foster used to laugh about this, and even now Foster smiled. Wasn't it ironic, how he was the one who had ended up in the city, and not Beckley?

Slowly he stopped walking to stare in at a display of Christmas ornaments. Yes, it was ironic, how things had worked out, how he was the one with his name on business cards.

An ugly thought reared its head and gave him the feeling that irony wasn't the word he was looking for. A shadow fell over his face in the sunlight. It's not that way, he thought. Here, I'll do a test.

When he next heard footsteps crunching down the sidewalk, he turned his head to look. There they were, the doll-like citizens, just as he'd seen them an hour ago. He imagined Beckley with meaningless eyes like theirs, and he winced, because he'd felt what he'd feared—a twinge of satisfaction.

Expiration Date

RONA WANG, Grade 12, Age 17. Lincoln High School, Portland, OR.
Emily Hensley, *Educator*

The house was too big for just Miriam and her mother, which was another way of saying it was too empty. Gone were the days when her mother would stand in the kitchen, making phone calls about things that needed fixing to people who would fix them—the plumber, the cable repairman, the marriage counselor. Now it was just the real estate agent, a sophisticated woman with silver jewelry and pearl-buttoned blouses and tasteful peach lipstick, and strings of interested buyers.

Miriam's mother was always at the office these days, so most evenings it was just Miriam making dinner for herself. She dug through the refrigerator, searching for maybe leftovers from the Thai place down the street, or milk to make instant mac-n-cheese from a box. Instead, she found the strawberries.

Both Miriam and her mother disliked the sour taste—Miriam had read somewhere once that a lemon had more sugar than a strawberry—but they were her father's favorite. White-green fuzz smothered the berries, disrupting the glimmering deep-red skin. Miriam didn't understand why her mother kept buying them and then pushing the cartons to the back of the refrigerator, hidden behind the milk and eggs and bread. Maybe it was just habit, or maybe something more.

Either way, Miriam couldn't bring herself to throw the moldy strawberries out, so she left them on the shelf and poured herself a bowl of Lucky Charms instead. She had homework and it was late and she was too exhausted to make anything substantial, plus her mother wasn't here to tell her no, and of course, her father wasn't here to say anything at all.

Before he left, her father had been working on the basement. It was a muggy and hot July, sticky like a fruit pit, and Miriam had felt very important standing next to him, snapping the bright-yellow tape measure between her fingers.

They were going to have a flat screen, he said. A forty-inch. Throw in leather couches, a small bar. Hardwood floors. They could invite all the neighbors to watch the Super Bowl together.

Miriam didn't like football much—in fact she wasn't even sure of the rules, but she had agreed anyway, and for a moment she had even believed him.

Their new apartment smelled like fresh paint. Miriam's room faced the street, and in the evenings she'd watch the sidewalks peel away to the crowds swelling and fizzing. Everybody always had somewhere to be. Each night, the buzz, the hunger of the city would echo and bounce, making it near impossible to sleep.

The noise filled up the emptiness. After all, when they moved in, they didn't bring any photos of Miriam's father. The place wasn't nearly big enough for ghosts.

The prospective buyers could always find something to complain about. The kitchen was too small, the basement was unfinished, this neighborhood wasn't in the best school district.

After she and her mother had moved out, Miriam came back to the house sometimes in the afternoons, just to soak in the white-gold light streaming in through the windows, glimmering with the possibility of what once was. Like picking at a scab after falling off her bike, she couldn't help it. The memories leaking through the walls until the air was dense and trembling.

Here was the mahogany staircase—when she was eight, she'd tried sliding down the railing and ended up in the emergency room with eight stitches on her bottom lip. Here was the bathtub where her mother had (unsuccessfully) tried to teach her how to swim—Miriam had complained about boredom until the water went cold, and then she'd instead complained about her inevitable death by hypothermia. Her father had chuckled, the sound full and expanding like a bright-red balloon. The next weekend, he took her to the lake.

It was on one of these days when Miriam was sitting on the staircase with her algebra homework spread out on her lap, just her and the stillness, when the front door clicked open.

The real estate agent swept in, along with a dark-haired man in his late twenties.

"This place is just the perfect size to start a family in," she was saying, and then stopped short when her eyes fell on Miriam. "Oh! Hello."

Miriam could feel her cheeks warming. She wasn't sure why, but it felt like she'd been caught red-handed stealing something that wasn't quite hers anymore. "I'm so sorry—I didn't know you were showing the house today—I'm not—you know—I'll go."

Quickly she gathered up her things and slipped through the door, meeting neither adult's eyes.

Sometime soon after, Miriam's mother told her that the dark-haired man and his new wife had decided to purchase. Settlement day came and went. A while after that, Miriam and her mother happened to pass by the house on their way to the grocery store. Usually, they'd take the car, but gas was expensive, and it was a nice sunny day out and exercise was good for the health.

Miriam wasn't about to complain; her mother had been mostly absent the last few months, and any time she got to spend with her remaining parent was precious. The dark-haired man, as well as a woman sporting a baby bump, were in the front yard gardening. They both waved.

Miriam's mother stopped for a bit of small talk—how were they, how far along was the baby, the weather was so lovely, wasn't it? Miriam watched the couple smile at each other, their eyes twinkling when they met, like the other person was the single brightest star in the galaxy.

But even stars burned out, Miriam knew. Her parents had smiled so genuinely at each other once, but love, like everything else, expired. When mold stains had first shown up, her father had tossed the entire thing away, including his own daughter.

Miriam's mother stopped, opened her mouth like maybe she was going to warn the newlyweds to be careful, that nothing came without an expiration date. But instead, all she did was congratulate them, wish them luck with the baby and a nice evening.

Later, at the grocery store, her mother didn't purchase any strawberries.

School for Gifted and Talented Secretly Run by Gay Mafia

VERONICA MARKS, Grade 11, Age 16. Hunter College High School, New York, NY. Kip Zegers, *Educator*

NEW YORK, NY—After a close examination of Oakwood Conservatory for the Gifted and Talented's funding, it was discovered on Monday that Oakwood is, in fact, run by the gay mafia. "Well, this explains a lot," sniffed The One Conservative Student at Every Liberal School Who Just Doesn't Get With the Program, raising his eyebrows and straightening his tie before meandering away. Parents, however, seemed far more surprised.

"I'm definitely surprised that Oakwood is run by the gay mafia, but I'm even more surprised that Oakwood isn't run by my child," declared one parent. "My Jimmy runs three clubs, gets nothing below an A, and plays the piano, and you're telling me the gay mafia runs this school? Does the gay mafia even play piano?"

In fact, when we asked members of the Oakwood community who they thought did run the school, the most-reported answers were "my child," "the corrupt and capitalist bureaucracy," and many terrified students who merely whispered "caffeine," staring at us with broken, hopeless eyes.

"My daughter is on the track team," insisted one mom in yoga pants jogging outside of a gluten-free bakery. "She stars in every single theater production and just wrote a novel." However, she may not have been an Oakwood parent, because we actually just asked her for directions. After she had finished telling us the plot of her daughter's novel, she hopped on a stationary bike and started pedaling in the middle of the street.

One Oakwood parent did comment: "Zanessa takes classes at Columbia University, won two science fairs, and speaks four languages. But she is going to Harvard now, so I understand why the gay mafia would have to take over." Zanessa's father's words came out somewhat mumbled because of the Harvard sweatshirt, Harvard baseball cap, Harvard sunglasses, and Harvard full-body HazMat suit he was wearing, but we managed to catch them.

"I donate a lot of money to this school," one woman told us haughtily. "I did not become the most successful gynecologist in White Brooklyn for the gay mafia to be able to give more money—Taylor Swift comes to me, OK? Did you hear that, gay mafia? Taylor Swift's vagina!"

However, despite the jealousy expressed by many prideful parents, very few members of the Oakwood community were actually able to tell us what the gay mafia is. I, for one, made the mistake of asking a frantic junior outside of a U.S. History classroom two minutes before last period.

"Is this going to be on the test?" she wailed. Her eyes were dejected, held open by fear. One single teardrop sprouted, like a depressed flower on the verge of parabolic bloom. Circles under her eyes indicated her debilitating lack of sleep, her eyeliner was smudged on her cheekbones like war paint, and her fingers were ticking in the hand that did not hold a Starbucks Redeye.

I did not look back.

We then chose to speak with the younger students.

"I love all of their songs," one seventh-grader told us, with a very dedicated look.

However, we ended up getting the answer from That Conservative Student at Every Liberal School, who authoritatively told us this: "It's like the mafia," he said knowingly. "But, you know, with a very dangerous agenda."

An Instruction Manual on How to Survive an Indian House Party

ISHAN WALIA, Grade 8, Age 13. The Elisabeth Morrow School, Englewood, NJ. Laura Khutorsky, *Educator*

The first thing you need to know about an Indian house party is who to avoid. Run away from anyone who is wearing too much red lipstick, because otherwise, by the time you are leaving, your face will be painted red. Another type of person to stay away from is the relative with a huge beard, because he will bear hug you to death. You should know there are a few people I like to call conscripters or recruiters. I call them that because they will drag you onto the dance floor and force you to dance while music from your grandparent's time or the '80s prevents you from hearing anything.

The second thing you will need to know about these parties is that there will be approximately 20 to 30 guests. There may be up to 50, but those are just the "guess who got a new pool?" parties. Approximately a fourth of those attending are moms working in the kitchen. Food is a very big part of the culture, and many are proud of their cooking; however, some should not be.

The third thing you need to know about these functions is to expect the "Look at me, I am cool" person (usually male). While he is not your enemy, he is not your friend either. This man has a booming, obnoxious voice that he uses to simultaneously complain about his stock portfolio while complimenting the *kadhi* (a dish I will never understand, hailing from northern India). He will try to engage you by asking if you have attained a significant other or by simply calling you and everyone around you "bigshot," "man," or "dude." It is important to note that these monikers will be pronounced with an elongated stress on the vowels.

Now while there are your enemies at the get-togethers, there are also your allies who understand your plight. One of these allies is the "other kid" (not gender specific). These kids may be a few years older or a few years younger than you and are almost never your age. The younger species is much more immature, while the older variant is more mentally on your level. Usually you must entertain the younger ones. The older ones create a learning hands-on experience and will help you with all the skills you have yet to master, like dodging the one aunt you don't like while managing to make yourself a whole plate of curry to satisfy your uncle.

After examining adults and high school students old enough to talk with them, you must consider the children at the event. As mentioned before, your younger counterparts are not yet your equal mental brethren; however, you will be spending the most time with them. You may be given the task of looking after these younger humanoids. However, this pain will usually be relinquished after they go to sleep. Some may think this means their maternal and paternal figures have sacrificed their fun to bring their children home early. If you think that, you are dead wrong. Instead, the partying adults set up a "sleep room" with a plethora of pajamas. At a certain predetermined time, one parent will escort the younger ones to the sleep room and then proceed to turn off the lights and slam the door shut.

There will be an awkward time in your party-attending life when you may come across a problem. You will consider yourself too mature for the sleeping room, but still unable to enjoy talking with adults for over two minutes (ages 11-15). In this awkward transition period, you will walk around while helping yourself to the wide variety of beverages, making sure not to pick up a bottle of half-drunken rum. Many look upon this time as a downside, but personally, I think of it as a great time to strategize for the next phase of the party, saying good-bye.

At most parties, good-byes take a long period of time; however, at an Indian house party, this process takes nearly four hours. It will be initiated by a woman, and then dismissed by another fellow member of her gender. The men usually never get involved in this stage. Then, one hour later, someone will bring up the good-bye, and it will get dismissed once again. Again a half hour later, and then fifteen minutes later, and then ten minutes later, until the hosts give in to their guests and let them leave. This will always happen after midnight, at least three hours after the first mention of good-bye.

WALDEN BOOKER, *Astronomical*, Grade 11, Age 16. North East
School of the Arts, San Antonio, TX. Jennifer Janak, *Educator*

A Letter From Your Urban Private School

NATHANIEL DUNN, Grade 11, Age 16. The Berkley Carroll School, Brooklyn, NY. Erika Drezner, *Educator*

Dear Students and Faculty,

With Black History Month and a school-wide focus on race shifting toward the civil rights movement on the horizon, the discomfort of many white students has come to our attention. In order to accommodate these students who are feeling overwhelmed by the lack of attention to their own struggles, we have created a new student group.

Righteous American Caucasians Incessantly Sharing Their Troubles, or RACISTT for short, will provide a safe space for white students to complain about their problems during a time in which a small part of the focus at this school has been away from them. With this in mind, we would like to encourage everyone interested to attend the meetings held by this new group.

In order to ensure that this will be an effective and safe space for all students, we have created a few brief and simple guidelines to determine which students will be eligible to join.

We expect that the requirements provided below will ensure that only those who RACISTT is directed toward helping will be in the group. This will allow for more open and comfortable conversations.

The following is a list of requirements for entry into RACISTT: Must be of the Caucasian race.

Must not have a first, middle, or last name that is too foreign (we wouldn't want other students to feel uncomfortable). Must be a practicing classist.

Must have parents whose net worth amounts to at least $2.5 million (don't lie, we will know). Must own at least seven pairs of shoes.

Must donate money to charity annually. However, you may only donate to charity if you are doing it to tell everyone that you donate money to charity. Must have at least one racial or ethnic bias.

Must pretend you are poor, even when it is obvious you aren't. Must constantly tell minorities that you "understand their struggle." Must feel as though everything at your school is unfair.

Must genuinely believe your life is harder than everyone else's.

Must have some sort of personal connection with the name of this group.

Those who fit the criteria are invited to the first meeting this Friday during lunch. Lattes and sushi will be provided. As we expect that about 95% of you will meet these requirements, the meeting will be held in the auditorium. For those who are not attending, there will be rap music and fast food in room 304. However, we ask that you do not bring drugs or related items into the room with you.

As usual, if you have any problems with the contents of this email, please let us know, as your feedback is always extremely appreciated.* We thank you in advance for your cooperation, and we look forward to many successful conversations, including hearing you complain about your problems in the West Village, Tribeca, Dumbo, and beyond.

Cheers,

Your school's RACISTT Committee

*Unless your family has significant financial value to this school or you are an athlete, don't expect your comments to warrant a change.

The New Constitution of They, the People

SØREN BREDBERG, Grade 10, Age 16. Waterhouse LA Academy, Los Angeles, CA. Kimberly Bredberg, *Educator*

Three election cycles and America was on the verge of collapse.
Donald Trump's Second Mexican-American War.
Kanye West's redesign of the U.S. currency.

Both dropping near-fatal straws to Uncle Sam's back. We needed a new leader. Not another narcissistic celebrity buffoon. I was going to be that somebody. I may have been just another face in the crowd, but I had a plan to mend that factoid. Still, Trump and Kanye, both being celebrities, presented an obvious dilemma. Time for celebrity apprentice 101.

I started my campaigning in Iowa, being optimistic about things. Optimistic, that is, until people heard what I had to say. I had three basic stances fueling my campaign: repairing our national debt, mending relations with Mexico, and putting our nation's founders back on our money. I just forgot one thing: all of America's vast populace supports President Kanye and the legacy of President Trump. I can't lead a campaign on my road to celebrity-hood in states that love the things I'm running against! My campaign came to a sudden screeching halt.

Kanye's approval ratings were through the roof. There must be a handful of people I could campaign with, but who are they? Without any supporters, I had no donors. Without any donors, I had no money. Without any money, I had to do everything by myself.

My road to celebrity status just turned into a grass roots, money-free campaign. I called almost every number in the yellow pages looking for that 1% who agreed with my platform. I dreaded the day the CNN polls were released, but that day eventually came. It was worse than I ever would've thought. President Kanye, running for his second term, had a nice solid 92% in the polls, followed by first female presidential hopeful Katy Perry with 7%. When they were released, I lost all hope in my campaign and my country. They, the people, cared more about Hollywood-branded names than substantives. But an idea came to mind, so I Googled it to make sure I got my facts straight.

What if I didn't need the people?

Electors actually know and care about foreign relations, economic distress, and the tenacity of the American dream. I may not need that celebrity status after all. I went back to Iowa, this time focusing less on the people. I knew these people didn't care about speeches I spouted to them. And this time I didn't have to care either. So I played Byzantine politics, pretending to be out here for the people but just eyeing those electors. The debates were a breeze. I talked to people who didn't care. Kanye rapped to people who weren't listening. Katy sang to people who didn't know the difference. I talked to the deaf some more and eventually hopped on my campaign Uber to go home. Didn't throw my plan off a bit. I had my electors. The majority swore to vote for me because they actually care about the words that come out of my mouth, not the words on my birth certificate. Of course, my one compromise was in my VP choice. I needed an insurance policy, even if it did make me a little nervous. I didn't have to care anymore. I could just sit back, relax, and wait until November 7th.

When that day eventually came, I was ready. I had, being the only hopeful who passed high school government, coaxed the majority of electors in almost every state to cast their vote for me. I was going to be the face of America. I sat back and watched my TV screen. Of course the news told it as it was. Kanye won the popular vote, with 99.9% of votes, Katy receiving 0.1%. I got none. But they had no idea what would happen next.

Introducing America's next president.

Thing is, I was the only one celebrating. With no supporters and no campaign team, I celebrated by myself. My inauguration day would most likely be the same, better start training now. I plopped on my couch and started drafting a speech that nobody would listen to. Unfortunately, I realized that about halfway through the crafting. I closed my computer and gave up, who would care anyway?

I fell asleep, but woke up with another belated realization. I was becoming one of them. I didn't have any policies. I had ignored them since my campaign U-turned. I decided I'd better write that speech after all. I hustled and spent about a week crafting a solid sing-song inaugural address. I dream of a better America, for the people etc., just the usual.

It was a short week. It was also a short couple of months until January 20th. With my speech in my pocket, I straightened my tie, pushed in my Old Glory lapel pin, and was ready to speak to a bunch of disgruntled Americans. The motorcade pulled into 1600 Pennsylvania Avenue. The sights were horrendous. It looked like I stepped out of reality and into a zombie flick. I took to the stage on the White House front lawn anyway, shocked by the presence of dissonance. I opened my mouth and was about to speak the first phrases of my stereotypical "change" speech. At that very moment, the Secret Service deemed the situation too dangerous and they pulled me offstage. I knew my vice president was just getting ready to say the oath instead of me. I almost broke out in tears—sad for where my nation had landed, sad for where it was headed.

I was being pushed into my limo, but I wanted to have one last sight of the pandemic of blindness. That's when I saw that this was not your average zombie flick. A face in the crowd locked eyes with mine. As I smiled, his eyes hardened, and his trained hands, too swift for my escorts, took aim. He was the feared lone wolf, Solitarius lupus, the one who lived to ensure America's continued decline. Mysteriously, my VP was able to make it away before the shots were fired. I never heard the shots, but as my field of vision narrowed to a pinpoint and everything turned to white, in my mind, I could hear my VP taking the oath that should have been mine. "I, President Cyrus do solemnly swear . . ."

Academic Loses Bar Fight Summarily and Decisively

BRANDON SCHRÖEDER, Grade 12, Age 18. Stanton College Preparatory, Jacksonville, FL. Larry Knight, *Educator*

Brantford Wentworth-MacDougal, a professor at a prestigious Massachusetts research university, was peeled off the floor of a nearby drinking establishment Wednesday night. This has been confirmed by Officer J.R. Fruitbat of the North Haverbrook Police Department.

The Ward S. Kaltenbrunner Professor of Fine Art, Media, and Culture at Alberts-Kettering University was loitering at the Vast Tracts Inn on November 4 of this year, partaking in what he describes as "an eventful evening filled with spirited bacchanalia."

According to Candice Whetstone, registered nurse, the professor sustained a series of grievous wounds. This combination of injuries left him bound to a wheelchair. He was dealt two broken legs, five broken ribs, two black eyes, a split lip, and a bruised ego by Colonel Charles "Chuck" Steak, a Vietnam veteran who self-identifies as a "crusty old man."

The two men were less than friendly before any physical

confrontation. They had already engaged in a series of grumbles and passive-aggressive sideways glances.

"When the professor asked the Colonel for his Myers-Briggs personality type, there was no turning back," said Murph Lovett, a local barfly. "Academic condescension is something the Colonel just can't stand."

Wentworth-MacDougal, who refers to himself as "a proud INTP," defended his line of questioning as "a perfectly reasonable counterweight to the typical clichés of barroom banter."

When the fight began at 11:38 p.m., each of the two combatants were noticeably intoxicated. In a two-hour span, Colonel Steak was up to nine-and-a-half beers, and the professor had imbibed six double Scotch whiskies.

"The evening's ethanol intake seemed appropriate enough," Wentworth-MacDougal said. "I was donning my special 'make-it-a-double' blazer that night. It's a resplendent green corduroy, complete with elbow patches and all the trimmings."

Colonel Steak, among other bar patrons, found the professor's unique garment offensive.

"Where I come from, people who wear things like that are just asking to get whooped. That jacket looked like it was stolen from the Salvation Army bin, and it smelled like it too," Steak said. "The icing on the cake came when the artsy little hipster weasel asked me something about a Michael Myers personality test. That's when I knew I had to open up a can of whoop-[expletive]."

The altercation can hardly be referred to as a "fight," per se, because the word implies that two people are participating. This incident was largely one-sided.

The squabble began with the Colonel hitting Wentworth-MacDougal directly in the throat with a solid right cross. From there, it only got worse. Steak broke both of the professor's legs with a high-heeled shoe and a two-by-four he found in a nearby gully.

There was still more pugilism to follow—Colonel Steak's final statement of the evening was a series of vicious rabbit punches to Wentworth-MacDougal's face and head. In the entire three minutes, the professor had only attempted a hilariously effeminate backhand, which didn't connect with anything but a barstool.

According to Mr. Lovett, the professor had attempted to resolve the conflict with humor. However, it was only escalated when he began yelping a series of elaborate, pretentious insults at Colonel Steak.

"He called me a 'ninnyhammer,'" Steak said. "After that he said I was a 'rube,' a 'guttersnipe,' and a 'simpleton who's too stupid to understand irony.' That last part isn't even true—I know exactly what irony is. It's that taste that's left in your mouth when you pick your teeth with a nail." The Colonel has just begun his fourth stint at Veterans' Affairs sensitivity training.

Professor Wentworth-MacDougal has decided not to press charges, although he stands in resolute defense of his actions that night.

"There's nothing wrong, per se, with a Jungian gallivant on a Wednesday night," he said. "Nietzsche and Dylan were both correct: The rabble shouldn't criticize what it can't understand."

RAZAN ELBABA, *American Role Models*, Grade 12, Age 17, Oakton High School, Vienna, VA. Susan Silva, *Educator*

ABOUT THE AUTHORS

BRITT ALPHSON writes because in its simplest form, life is really just a beautiful and messy collection of intertwining stories—and she wants her verse, no matter how small, to mean something.

Unlike most poets, MARGOT ARMBRUSTER is surprisingly not addicted to coffee. In her spare time, she studies Latin and Catullus's poetry, which reminds her that—despite the state of disarray her life is continually in—she is not the least stable poet in history.

STELLA BINION has been writing before she could write, telling her mom to jot down her words on scraps of paper from the age of three. Today, Stella is a member of the performance poetry group Rebirth Poetry Ensemble and spends most of her time riding Chicago's public transportation and wearing big earrings.

RYLEE BLACK has too many books to fit her shelf, and the wall above her bed is covered with hand-drawn medical diagrams and her favorite works of art. She always wears friendship bracelets until the threads break.

DANIEL BLOKH (the coolest kid on the Blokh) writes only because it makes his parents think he's working. He has a lifetime supply of worry, far too many copies of Allen Ginsberg's *Howl*, and a beautiful painting of Ron Swanson. What he doesn't have is any idea what he's doing.

CARISSA CHEN writes because she grew up with a lisp and poetry gave her a voice. Living in Shanghai and a small California town made her realize how silence can be dangerous or boring. She has moved seven times, likes writing her poetry with different colored pens, and is convinced she has synesthesia.

SADIE COWLES enjoys writing, loves books, and has been known to read a book a day for weeks at a time. She also loves playing the fast-paced card game called Nerts, swimming in the cold Maine ocean (even in the winter), and baking chocolate cakes.

ALINE DOLINH has been described by others as a 'lunchbox witch,' 'sorority goth,' and 'caffeine slave.' Her favorite genres of anything are sci-fi, horror, and romantic comedy, and she's still hoping to write something that features all three at once.

Every morning, **AMY DONG** enjoys a bowl of Greek yogurt topped with fruits of Foster Wallace's wit, granola of Vonnegut's skepticism, and honey of life's sweet joys. She switches flavors every day to make sure no two mornings are the same.

KATHERINE DU is a columnist for *The Huffington Post* and a contributing writer for *USA TODAY*. She writes to unearth the gorgeous wounds of memory. After taking a gap year to fathom, create, and love as much as she can, she will attend Stanford University in fall 2017.

AMY DUNCAN is still trying to figure out what's what and who's who, so most of her poetry is about identity as an individual and a collective. When she's not writing, she spends her time studying vegetarian recipes and stretching her legs (and her budget) at the local mall.

Although **NATHANIEL DUNN** has spent his seventeen plus years of life residing in Brooklyn, he will likely spend eternity in hell—at least if the targets of his writing have a say. When Nathaniel finally realized that sharing one's judgments about the world vocally is something reserved for crazed people on New York City subways, he turned to writing.

MAYA EASHWARAN is a violinist and poet who loves chocolate a little too much. She enjoys doodling pointlessly and is currently obsessed with *Hamilton,* the musical. She loves poetry because of its rhythmic qualities and its ability to connect people.

DAVID EHMCKE is on a mission to visit every coffee shop in Iowa City, where he is currently studying at the University of Iowa. Much of his recent writing has been inspired by a workshop prompt: "Write about an experience you will never be able to understand." Above all, David wants to learn about your current Netflix binge.

JACKSON EHRENWORTH is a city boy who spends his spare time on icy heights with calamitous possibilities. He writes to tackle unfairness, to disrupt certitude, and to occupy even a moment in the company of others who love words. He is currently preoccupied with dismantling convictions of the supremacy of the five-paragraph essay.

AVA GOGA is a poet-artist from Reno, Nevada. Perhaps their greatest accomplishment is being able to sometimes keep houseplants alive. They believe in extraterrestrial life, eating breakfast for dinner, and you.

Hailing from Connecticut, **ASHLEY GONG** is a lover of puns, wordplay, and anything linguistic. Besides enjoying poetry, she likes reading ancient Latin texts, playing flute, and skiing whenever she can. Her favorite writers include Ocean Vuong and Frank O'Hara.

ADAM GOWAN converts his thoughts into words as a way to navigate his emotional landscape and to seek answers to the philosophical questions the events of his life constantly present. Writing is a way of giving physical form to the intangible—and revealing the connection between all human beings.

Growing up, **ALEXANDRA GULDEN**'s family did not often tell stories about their past, so she decided to create her own. "What Latino family doesn't think it's cursed?" Junot Díaz once wrote, and she tries to incorporate this belief in her own writing.

KEVIN HELOCK started his career in the best way possible: completely ignoring his teachers and reading under the desk. When he's not writing, he's sobbing his eyes out at only the most emotional of video games, or teaching youths the potentially dangerous skills of knot-tying and fire-building at scout camp.

ANGELO HERNANDEZ-SIAS is a writer who makes beats and raps to them. Writers (Kendrick Lamar, Toni Morrison, Junot Díaz, Chimamanda Ngozi Adichie) have reminded him that he is human even when dominant narratives have told him otherwise. He writes to remind people of their humanity.

HENRY HICKS began writing at a young age, often jotting down silly stories of dragons and clones. Today, he writes fiction pieces, dabbling in most genres, along with poetry. He is involved in school theater and enjoys photography. His writing is influenced by that of Andrew Smith, Matthew Quick, and Allen Ginsberg.

ALLISON JIANG is a perpetual mess, but she likes to write. She hopes to one day own a big dog, play with words for a living, and hold the Guinness World Record for most television watched by a human person.

When **DANIEL KALUS** wants something done, it needs to be done yesterday. Witty, charming, confident, energetic, exuberant, creative. None of these words have been uttered by Daniel Kalus, but all describe him to a "t." Daniel's writing style is geared toward film, with an interest in possibly being a director some day.

CAMERON KELLEY is a Leo, a lover of socks, a believer that avocados should have their own food group, and, according to a Buzzfeed quiz, if she were a type of potato dish, she'd be latkes. She writes about love, because it's important and the world is full of it, and about werewolves, because werewolves are super cool.

LUC LAMPIETTI is an avid procrastinator with a dorm room that makes B. Sullivan's apartment look like a page out of an IKEA catalogue. When he's not brushing things off, he likes to write about people lazier and more debauched than him.

ANNA LANCE's superpower is never getting carsick. Many hours of reading while traveling were necessary to discover and hone her ability, which she now puts to use stacking words in airplanes and on horses as a National Student Poet (class of 2015).

If you have never met **NIA LARTEY**, be cautious, as she is 1,000,000 times louder and more talkative than the rest of the human population. Though she's been writing most of her life, she credits her seventh-grade English teacher, Mr. Carroll, for the Nia who writes today.

JENNIFER LEE loves Emily Dickinson, pistachio ice cream, and thinking about the consumption of women in popular culture. Sometimes, she still finds herself in awe of the fact that humans can use writing as a means of communication. She will attend Columbia University next fall.

VIDHISHA MAHESH has many weaknesses, the most prominent of which include peanut M&Ms, white choco-chip cookies from Costco, and the urge to include food-related self-deprecation in personal bios to increase overall likability.

VERONICA MARKS loves all forms of storytelling, like acting, singing, and reading the news out loud (kidding!), but she especially likes writing, because it is the creation of the story itself. She genuinely hopes you have a great day.

SOPHIA MAUTZ thinks in stanzas. She finds transcendence in nature and seeks to synthesize these experiences with words, acting as both a voice that speaks for the natural world, and one that calls us to commune with it.

RUOHAN MIAO writes because there is nothing more satisfying than building new worlds and characters. When she is not staring blankly at an empty Word document, she watches unrealistic police procedurals and medical dramas.

KATIE MLINEK is a writer, filmmaker, and croissant-craving ginger from Baltimore, MD. She writes so that she can immortalize life in case we all become robots someday and forget how to feel. She is currently working on procuring a pool filled with chocolate—it would go great with croissants.

RACHEL PAGE is a writer, twin, and avid Netflix watcher who has lived for eighteen years in the nation's capital. She will be attending Columbia University in the fall.

JENNIFER PARK took up writing because if no one cared for what she had to say now, maybe they would care for what she had to say later. She is also the proud owner of a very large stuffed penguin and an 1830s fashion sense.

NOEL PENG is a tiny human. Her first short story was a plagiarized version of *Cloudy With a Chance of Meatballs*, which her first-grade self was very proud of until she realized this was not OK. She started writing because she realized it was an activity that was very easy to keep secret from her parents (shh...).

VASANTHA SAMBAMURTI is an Indian girl from the South. She pronounces her name three different ways depending on whom she's speaking to. She enjoys listening to soulful tunes, finding work by artists of color, and eating pomegranates.

AVIK SARKAR, poet and composer, voices his ideas through words and notes. Inspired by e.e. cummings, M.I.A., Tumblr, and the Geeta, he's compelled to write because it's the most polite way to vent.

Above all, **BRANDON SCHRÖEDER** aspires to be "the Richard Feynman of literature." He likes to laugh, so he writes mostly satirical columns and silly short stories. He is presently focusing his attention on how to become a postmodern existentialist and prepare a five-star trout almondine.

PARISA THEPMANKORN writes in the hopes that people will use it to distinguish her from her twin sister. Other than writing, her favorite hobbies include breakfast, lunch, and dinner—and of course, Instagramming pictures of it all.

SAMANTHA TIMMERS spent most of her childhood thinking up questions such as "What would you do if a man-sized duck attacked you?" She's since learned that she's better off writing about the possibilities instead. Samantha will be attending the University of Louisville to find out more answers to important life-altering questions.

Currently slogging through adolescence, **AMELIA VAN DONSEL** can be found in empty rooms with a lot of paper or trekking the Massachusetts woods. Habits include setting the microwave for odd amounts of time, correcting the grammar of strangers, and refusing eBooks.

PEYTON VASQUEZ is a swimmer, writer, comedian, runner, weight lifter, entertainer, and overall good guy. He is much more than a radioactive cancer survivor who is inspired by other patients' stories and the volunteers who work tirelessly to improve the lives of children with life-threatening illnesses.

When he was a young child, **ISHAN WALIA** never knew what his "thing" was. Then, in 5th grade, he tried out something called writing. Within 30 seconds he realized that he had found, his "thing." Since that day, Ishan has been constantly inspired by the beautiful world around him.

JULIA WALTON's stories seek to capture universal moments of the human experience. Her favorite author is Ursula Le Guin, and her favorite poet is Edna St. Vincent Millay. She hopes that one day, her stories will make everyone who reads them a little kinder. For now, it's enough if you like them.

RONA WANG loves cats even though she's allergic to them, listens to K-pop even though she can't understand most of the lyrics, and writes even though she kant spel. She is inspired by bad reality television, food, and upcoming deadlines. In the fall, she will attend the Massachusetts Institute of Technology.

ADRIANA WATKINS began her writing career as a six-year-old who told stories about talking cats. Now she writes about people, because that target audience is more literate. She hopes to publish something good before she gets so old that she wants to write about cats again.

If not hibernating in 12-hour cycles or eating out of boredom, **SYDNI WELLS** spends much of her time doing what every other teenager does: having an existential crisis. Occasionally you can find her attempting to be self-aware and intellectual, which she sometimes calls poetry.

DANIEL WU enjoys many things—free food, funky friends, and a fair world. Armed with voice and volition, wit and whimsy, stomach and satire, he longs to travel the world and challenge the complacency of the status quo. He hopes the world will surpass him in that regard.

ALISHA YI attributes her writing to the fact that she wasn't born with a silver spoon in her mouth. Her life is a plume of thoughts made on a whim—her go-to source for inspiration. And when she isn't writing, she goes on dicey excursions to find a way to be listened to.

Journalism to **MINA YUAN** is a fantastic excuse to stick her nose in everyone's business. Her favorite authors include Truman Capote and Michael Pollan, and her ideal world includes a perfectly accurate interview-transcribing machine.

ALEX ZHANG spent a majority of his childhood pondering the age-old question of what rhymes with orange. In ten years, he hopes to be found in New York with his photography on the covers of *Vogue* and his poetry on the shelves of bookstores. He will be attending Columbia University in the fall.

JESSICA ZHANG writes because of art. She writes because of the news, or because of the moon. She writes as a means of inquiry, and because it is a way of changing a life without changing out of pajamas.

EDUCATORS LIST

Charlotte Agell
Harrison Middle School
Yarmouth, ME

Cheri Anderson
Roncalli High School
Aberdeen, SD

Sara Bauer
Morris Hills High School
Rockaway, NJ

Alex Berg
Hunter College High School
New York, NY

Sarah Blackman
Fine Arts Center
Greenville, SC

Kimberly Bredberg
Waterhouse LA Academy
Los Angeles, CA

Samuel Brown
Miami Country Day School
Miami, FL

Wendy Bryce
East High School
Sioux City, IA

Mercedes Carbonell
Phillips Exeter Academy
Exeter, NH

Kirk Carlson
Muskegon High School
Muskegon, MI

Phyllis Carr
Hamilton High School
Chandler, AZ

Linda Carswell
St. John's School
Houston, TX

Betsey Coleman
Colorado Academy
Denver, CO

Denise Croker
The Harpeth Hall School
Nashville, TN

Kathy Crutcher
Woodrow Wilson High School
Washington, D.C.

Norma DaCrema
Academy of Notre Dame de
Namur
Villanova, PA

Steven Dante
Holmdel High School
Holmdel, NJ

Danielle DeTiberus
Charleston County School of
the Arts
North Charleston, SC

Erin Dolias
Home School
New York, NY

Erika Drezner
The Berkley Carroll School
Brooklyn, NY

Joe Forsyth
Penn Wood High School
Landsdowne, PA

Suzy Fox
Delta High School
Muncie, IN

Cheryl Fritz
Ephrata High School
Ephrata, PA

Daniel Gray-Kontar
Cleveland School of the Arts
High School
Cleveland, OH

Ashley Gore
Scott High School
Taylor Mill, KY

David Griffith
Interlochen Arts Academy
Interlochen, MI

Kate Hackett
Marymount High School Los
Angeles
Los Angeles, CA

Grace Hamilton
Polytechnic School
Pasadena, CA

Marea Haslett
Milton High School
Alpharetta, GA

Todd Hearon
Phillips Exeter Academy
Exeter, NH

Emily Hensley
Lincoln High School
Portland, OR

Rebecca Ingerslev
Westford Academy
Westford, MA

Thomas Kane
Phillips Academy
Andover, MA

Kevin Kearney
Waltham Senior High School
Waltham, MA

Laura Khutorsky
The Elisabeth Morrow School
Englewood, NJ

Franz Klein
St. Thomas More Academy
Raleigh, NC

Larry Knight
Stanton College Preparatory
Jacksonville, FL

Dana Mayfield
University School of Nashville
Nashville, TN

Tiffany Melanson
Douglas Anderson School of
the Arts
Jacksonville, FL

Catherine Melton
Timber Creek High School
Orlando, FL

Daniel Mendel
Avenues: The World School
New York, NY

Kelly Miller
Platte City Middle School
Platte City, MO

Mamie Morgan
South Carolina Governor's
School for the Arts and
Humanities
Greenville, SC

Nicholas Morgan
Etobicoke School of the Arts
Toronto, Canada

Victoria Nordlund
Rockville High School
Rockville, CT

Sara Peck
University School of the
Lowcountry
Mount Pleasant, SC

Ashley Perez
School of the Arts
Rochester, NY

Donna Pilgrim
The Village School
Houston, TX

Brad Richard
Lusher Charter School
New Orleans, LA

Iris Rinke-Hammer
Alabama School of Fine Arts
Birmingham, AL

Alan Rossi
South Carolina Governor's
School for the Arts and
Humanities
Greenville, SC

Leslie Russell
Payton College Preparatory
High School
Chicago, IL

Karen Schleicher
Brookfield Academy
Brookfield, WI

Jeff Schwartz
Greenwich Academy
Greenwich, CT

Veronica Serna
Bonnette Junior High School
Deer Park, TX

Kacie Shingara
Folsom High School
Folsom, CA

Susan Sullivan
Oakton High School
Vienna, VA

Suzanne Supplee
George Washington Carver
Center for Arts and
Technology
Towson, MD

Talin Tahajian
The Adroit Journal Summer
Mentorship Program
Philadelphia, PA

Temperance Tinker
West High School
Anchorage, AK

Miles Trump
Wayzata High School
Plymouth, MN

Michelle Toby
Newtown High School
Sandy Hook, CT

LuAnn Underwood
Harborside Academy
Kenosha, WI

Paula Uriarte
Capital High School
Boise, ID

Angie Van Berckelaer
Olympus High School
Salt Lake City, UT

Melissa Villanueva
Ed W. Clark High School
Las Vegas, NV

Anne Wagenhals
Castilleja School
Palo Alto, CA

Tonya Walker
St. Catherine's School
Richmond, VA

Richard Weems
Bergen County Academies
Hackensack, NJ

Wes Williams
Buckingham Browne &
Nichols School
Cambridge, MA

Lily Windle
Lincoln High School
Portland, OR

Kip Zegers
Hunter College High School
New York, NY

AN EDUCATOR'S GUIDE TO *THE BEST TEEN WRITING OF 2016*

Use the works of these award-winning teen writers to inspire discussion and guide writing exercises with students.

1. Short Story: Discussion on characterization and voice—35 minutes

Goal: Students explain how authors establish the voice of a narrator to create distinct characters who inform a reader of time, place, and mood.

Activity: Introduce the concept of a story's "voice" by having students discuss popular first-person narratives as well as close third-person narratives that are particularly different and compelling.

Next, choose a piece with highly engaging character voice(s). As you're reading out loud, have students mark any points in the text where they notice specific character establishment through the tone of the prose, dialects, slang, humor, or other details. After you're finished, have students discuss the following:

• What does the author want us to know or understand about the narrator of this story?

• How does the separation of character voices establish a reliable—or unreliable—narrator?

Have students, in partners or groups, select a narrator and describe his or her personality. Then have them return to the text and find specific details (speech, thought, and interaction with others) to illustrate the narrator's personality and how it informs and shapes the narrative. Share student responses.

2. Short Story: Writing with focus on characterizing the narrative—35 minutes

Goal: Students restructure a narrative with another narrator, creating the same story with a different perspective.

Activity: Ask students to take on the voice of one of the other characters and tell the story from that point of view, filling in blanks that the original narrator did not. Challenge students to use important characterizing details in the reading to give color to their entries.

3. Poetry: Writing with focus on form—30 minutes

Goal: Students write using different structural techniques.

Activity: Have students write two poems on one topic of their choosing. Begin with a prose poem, in which they write freely on that topic; then have them write another poem on the same topic with a focus on line breaks to emphasize changes in rhythm or highlight specific phrases. Discuss the differences after sharing the results.

4. Personal Essay/Memoir: Writing with a focus on structure and pacing—45 minutes

Goal: Students will write an organized and coherent memoir imitating the format of a *Best Teen Writing* piece.

Activity: Select a personal essay/memoir from the anthology to read out loud with your students. Talk about the format in which the memoir is written. Discuss the choices made and how those choices are inherently personal, therefore inherently suited to convey a personal essay.

Ask your students to write their own memoir modeled after the memoir you have selected. Have the students share their work and discuss choices that each student makes, including how those choices convey something personal to the reader.

5. Genre-Shifting Exercise: 40 minutes

Goal: Students will explore form's relationship to function by converting a piece in the anthology to another genre. For example, reimagine a play as a poem; a personal essay/memoir as a science fiction/fantasy piece.

Activity: Have the students choose a favorite piece in *The Best Teen Writing*, then have them reinterpret that work in another genre. Afterward, have the students compare the original to the genre-shifted piece and discuss how the same information is relayed through contrasting forms.

6. Blog Exercise: 40 minutes and homework time

Goal: Students will use critical-thinking skills to offer critiques and analysis of specific works or the anthology as a whole.

Activity: Ask students to write a blog post expressing thoughts about a specific piece of their choosing. Posts will be sent to the Alliance for consideration to be included on the Alliance blog.

• Students should express their opinions, offering positive feedback or constructive criticism, on a specific work in *The Best Teen Writing*. Alternatively, they may discuss the anthology as a whole.

• Posts may be emailed to **info@artandwriting.org**, with the subject line "The Best Teen Writing of 2016 Student Blog Post."

Educators: Continue the discussion! Explore with your peers even more ways in which *The Best Teen Writing of 2016* can inspire students in your classroom! Visit the Vision and Voice website, presented by the National Writing Project, at **visionandvoice.nwp.org** to learn more.

REGIONAL AFFILIATE ORGANIZATIONS

The Alliance's reach stems from our work with Affiliate Partner organizations that administer hundreds of art and/or writing regions across the country. They are responsible for bringing the Awards to local communities, educators, and students. It is because of our Affiliate Partners' extraordinary dedication that the Scholastic Awards have been able to reach more participants and provide additional opportunities for creative teenagers across the country.

NORTHEAST
Connecticut
Connecticut Art Region
Connecticut Art Education Association

Delaware
Delaware Art Region
Arts Center/Gallery at Delaware State University

Delaware Writing Region
Diamond State Branch, National League of American Pen Women, Inc.

District of Columbia
DC Metro Writing Region
Writopia Lab D.C.

Maine
Maine Art Region
Maine College of Art

Southern Maine Writing Region
The Southern Maine Writing Project at the University of
Southern Maine

Massachusetts
Massachusetts Art & Writing Region
School of the Museum of Fine Arts, Boston
The Boston Globe

New Hampshire
New Hampshire Art Region
The New Hampshire Art Educators' Association

New Hampshire Writing Region
The National Writing Project in New Hampshire
Plymouth State University

New Jersey
Northeast New Jersey Art Region
Montclair Art Museum

New York
Central New York Art Region
CNY Art Council, Inc.

Hudson Valley Art Region
Hudson Valley Art Awards
Sullivan, Dutchess, Orange, and Ulster County BOCES;
Enlarged City School District of Middletown; Orange County
Arts Council; Rolling V Transportation Services

Hudson-to-Housatonic Writing Region
Writopia Lab Westchester & Fairfield

New York City Art Region
Alliance for Young Artists & Writers
Parsons School of Design

New York City Writing Region
Alliance for Young Artists & Writers
Eugene Lang College of Liberal Arts

Pennsylvania
Berks, Carbon, Lehigh, and Northampton Art Region
East Central PA Scholastic Art Awards

Lancaster County Art Region
Lancaster Museum of Art

Lancaster County Writing Region
Lancaster Public Library

Northeastern Pennsylvania Art & Writing Region
Marywood University

Philadelphia Art Region
Philadelphia Arts in Education Partnership at the University
of the Arts

Philadelphia Writing Region
Philadelphia Writing Project

Pittsburgh Art Region
North Allegheny School District & Community College of
Allegheny County

Pittsburgh Writing Region
Western PA Writing Project

South Central Pennsylvania Art & Writing Region
Commonwealth Connections Academy

Southwestern Pennsylvania Art & Writing Region
California University of Pennsylvania

Rhode Island
Rhode Island Art Region
Rhode Island Art Education Association

Vermont
Vermont Art & Writing Region
Brattleboro Museum & Art Center

MIDWEST
Illinois
Chicago Writing Region
Chicago Area Writing Project

Mid-Central Illinois Art Region
Regional Scholastic Awards Council of Mid-Central Illinois

Suburban Chicago Art Region
Downers Grove North and South High Schools

Southern Illinois Art Region
John R. and Eleanor R. Mitchell Foundation
Cedarhurst Center for the Arts

Indiana
Central/Southern Indiana Art & Writing Region
Clowes Memorial Hall, Butler University, and Hoosier Writing Project at IUPUI

Kansas
Eastern Kansas Art Region
The Wichita Center for the Arts

Western Kansas Art Region
The Western Kansas Scholastic Art Awards

Michigan
Michigan Thumb Art Region
College for Creative Studies

Southeastern Michigan Art Region
College for Creative Studies

West Central Michigan Art & Writing Region
Kendall College of Art and Design, Ferris State University

Minnesota
Minnesota Art Region
Art Educators of Minnesota

Missouri
Missouri Writing Region
Greater Kansas City Writing Project

Nebraska
Nebraska Art Region
Omaha Public Schools Art Department

North Dakota
North Dakota Art Region
Plains Art Museum and the Red River Valley Writing Project
at NDSU

North Dakota Writing Region
The Red River Valley Writing Project at NDSU and
Plains Art Museum

Ohio
Central Ohio Art Region
Columbus College of Art & Design

Cuyahoga County Art & Writing Region
The Cleveland Institute of Art

Lorain County Art Region
Lorain County Regional Scholastic Arts Committee

Miami Valley Art Region
K12 Gallery & TEJAS

Northeast Central Ohio Art Region
Kent State University at Stark

Northeastern Ohio Art Region
Youngstown State University and Akron Children's Hospital
Mahoning Valley

South Dakota
South Dakota Art & Writing Region
The University of South Dakota

Wisconsin
Southeast Wisconsin Scholastic Writing Region
Southeast Wisconsin Scholastic Writing Region

Wisconsin Art Region
The Milwaukee Art Museum

Wisconsin Writing Region
Still Waters Collective

SOUTHEAST

Florida

Broward Art Region
Young at Art Museum

Hillsborough Art & Writing Region
Hillsborough County Public Schools

Miami-Dade Art Region
Miami-Dade County Public Schools

Miami-Dade Writing Region
Miami Writes

Northeast Florida Art Region
Northeast Florida Art Education Association

Palm Beach Art Region
Educational Gallery Group (Eg2)

Pinnellas Art Region
Pinellas County Art Region

Sarasota Art Region
Sarasota County Schools

Georgia

Georgia Art & Writing Region
Savannah College of Art and Design

Kentucky

Louisville Metropolitan Area Art Region
Jefferson County Public Schools

Northern Kentucky Writing Region
Northern Kentucky Writing Region

South Central Kentucky Art Region
Southern Kentucky Performing Arts Center (SKyPAC)

Mississippi

Mississippi Art Region
Mississippi Museum of Art

Mississippi Writing Region
The Eudora Welty Foundation

North Carolina

Eastern/Central North Carolina Art Region
Barton College

Mid-Carolina Art & Writing Region
Charlotte-Mecklenburg Schools

Western North Carolina Art Region
Asheville Art Museum

Tennessee

Middle Tennessee Art Region
Cheekwood Botanical Garden and Museum of Art

Virginia

Arlington County Art Region
Arlington County Public Schools

Fairfax County Art Region
Fairfax County Public Schools

Southwest Virginia Art Region
The Fine Arts Center for the New River Valley

SOUTHWEST
Arizona
Arizona Art & Writing Region
Young Authors of Arizona

Louisiana
North-Central Louisiana Writing Region
Northwestern State University Writing Project

Southeast Louisiana Writing Region
Greater New Orleans Writing Project

New Mexico
New Mexico Art Region
New Mexico Art Education Association

Oklahoma
Oklahoma Art Region
Tulsa Community College Liberal Arts Department

Texas
Harris County Art & Writing Region
Harris County Department of Education

San Antonio Art Region
SAY Sí (San Antonio Youth Yes)

Travis County Art Region
St. Stephen's School

West Texas Art Region
Wayland Baptist University and the Abraham Family
Art Gallery

WEST
Alaska
Alaska Art & Writing Region
Young Emerging Artists, Inc.

Colorado
Colorado Art Region
Colorado Art Education Association

Hawaii
Hawaii Art Region
Hawaii State Department of Education

Idaho
Idaho Writing Region
Boise State Writing Project

Nevada
Northern Nevada Art Region
The Nevada Museum of Art

Southern Nevada Art & Writing Region
Springs Preserve

Oregon
Oregon Art Region—Central Oregon Area
Oregon Art Education Association

Oregon Art Region—Portland Metro Area
Oregon Art Education Association

Oregon Art Region—Willamette Valley Art Region
Oregon Art Education Association and Benton
County Museum

Washington
Snohomish County Art Region
Schack Art Center

Washington State Art & Writing Region
Cornish College of the Arts

MULTI-STATE REGIONS
Iowa Multi-State Art & Writing Region
The Connie Belin & Jacqueline N. Blank International Center
for Gifted Education and Talent Development, University
of Iowa

Mid-South Art Region
Memphis Brooks Museum of Art

Northeast Indiana and Northwest Ohio Art & Writing Region
Fort Wayne Museum of Art

Northwest Indiana and Lower Southwest Michigan
Art Region
South Bend Museum of Art

Southern Ohio, Northern Kentucky, and Southeastern
Indiana Art Region
Art Academy of Cincinnati

Twin Tiers Art Region
Arnot Art Museum

ACKNOWLEDGEMENTS

The Alliance for Young Artists & Writers gratefully acknowledges the thousands of educators who encourage students to submit their works to the Scholastic Art & Writing Awards each year and the remarkable students who have the courage to put their art and writing before panels of renowned jurors. We would like to especially recognize the National Writing Project for its far-reaching efforts in the writing community and its continued commitment to our program. In addition, our mission is greatly furthered through special partnerships with the National Writing Project, National Art Education Association, the Association of Independent Colleges of Art and Design, and the NAACP's ACT-SO program.

THANK YOU TO OUR SPONSORS

Special thanks to: Scholastic Inc., the Maurice R. Robinson Fund, Command Web Offset Co., *The New York Times*, The Herb Block Foundation, Blick Art Materials & Utrecht Art Supply, the Royal Bank of Canada, Golden Artist Colors, Bloomberg Philanthropies, the Lily Auchincloss Foundation, the ESA Foundation, Neiman Marcus, the National Endowment for the Arts, the Gedenk Movement, the New York City Department of Cultural Affairs, Kramer Levin Naftalis & Frankel LLP; numerous other individual, foundation, and corporate funders; and, for the National Student Poets Program, the Institute of Museum and Library Services and the President's Committee on the Arts and the Humanities.

SUPPORT THE SCHOLASTIC ART & WRITING AWARDS

Help support the Awards today! Your support will go a long way toward making the Scholastic Awards available for future generations of creative teens. Visit **artandwriting.org/donate** to make a tax-deductible contribution online, or send your gift to Alliance for Young Artists & Writers, 557 Broadway, New York, NY 10012. Thank you!